Something I Said?

Something I Said?

Innuendo and Out the Other

Michael Feldman

Illustrations by
John Sieger

Music CD by
Michael Feldman and John Sieger

THE UNIVERSITY OF WISCONSIN PRESS
TERRACE BOOKS

The University of Wisconsin Press
1930 Monroe Street
Madison, Wisconsin 53711

www.wisc.edu/wisconsinpress/

3 Henrietta Street
London WC2E 8LU, England

1   3   5   4   2

Printed in the United States of America

Library of Congress Cataloging-in-Publication Data
Feldman, Michael, 1949–
Something I said? : innuendo and out the other /
Michael Feldman;
illustrations by John Sieger;
music CD by Michael Feldman and John Sieger.
p.   cm.
ISBN 0-299-20270-4 (alk. paper)
1. American wit and humor.   I. Sieger, John.   II. Title.
PN6165.F45   2004
814′.54—dc22   2004008109

Terrace Books, a division of the University of Wisconsin Press,
takes its name from the Memorial Union Terrace, located
at the University of Wisconsin–Madison. Since its inception in 1907,
the Wisconsin Union has provided a venue for students, faculty, staff,
and alumni to debate art, music, politics, and the issues of the day.
It is a place where theater, music, drama, dance, outdoor activities,
and major speakers are made available to the campus and the community.
To learn more about the Union, visit www.union.wisc.edu.

For ELLIE
and
NORA

With love, and thanks for all the material

Contents

Contents

VI I Was Just Thinking

Acknowledgments

My thanks to the Milwaukee and Madison Feldmans, especially, of course, David A. and Geraldine G. (who deserve a fund in their names just like the MacArthurs), and my brothers Clay, How, and Art, who covered the professions so that I didn't have to, and, of course, my inspirations, Ellie, Nora, and their matriarch, Sandy; my former students in Kenosha and Madison, who seem to be doing well despite my instruction; Jack Mitchell, erstwhile head of Wisconsin Public Radio and the only man to put me on the air and not yank me off; my radio audience, those supportive and wonderful people who, for reasons known only to themselves, come to see a radio show; my co-conspirators on *Whad'ya Know?*, Jim, John, Jeff, Lyle, Stephen, Rick, Todd, Judith, Kelly, Carrie, Curt, and the very funky Clyde; and my collaborator and longest-running relationship, John Sieger, for his friendship and his music, and for the cartoons that dot this book, which, Nora says, look nothing like me, but still.

 Introduction

I'm not essentially a writer (they're born, like jockeys), but this being America, at least until further notice, I don't think that should stop me from writing a book. They say everyone has a book in them; what they don't say is that, in almost all cases, "in them" is where it's better left. Not having anything to say has never stopped anyone from saying it; hence, *Something I Said?*, a collection of things I have written despite knowing that, should I squeeze out another book, it would be punished by a book tour and rewarded with disappointing sales despite an overflow crowd at the Little Professor in King-of-Prussia PA, and genuine excitement in the Quad Cities. Radio is so much easier than writing: you say things and they go away, and, if not, you deny them. It's a stream of lack of consciousness, an opportunity for an individual who, under ordinary circumstances, would be the last to share, to come forth with the very things he was right not to voice. It's ear candy; unlike an infinite number of monkeys, an infinite number of guys on the radio would never write Shakespeare, or even say anything very memorable (Fred Allen excepted). How many times has someone come up to me and offered, "What you said on the air today was really great" (pause). "What was it?" I can never remember, either. This is the thing I hear most often from the public in public radio—along with my other favorite thing, usually from young women, which is that their mothers (and, increasingly, their grannies) *love* me. The remedy, setting those very same ill-thought-out remarks down on paper, requires that they be thought about, and it's hard to maintain consistent ill thinking through several rewrites of what was essentially an off-the-cuff crack of no great import, anyway. But, anyway, I've tried, and here they are in *Something I Said?* Buy me a beer sometime, and I'll slur a few very similar, if not identical, points of view. I hope your grannie *loves* this.

I

A House of
a Guy's Own

A House of a Guy's Own

Fall is coming to A House of a Guy's Own, time to think about raising the wheels on the mower to attempt one last pass through the thatch, maybe doing something with the flowers—but what? They seem to grow back, regardless, so they must be perennials. The natural yard needs a woman's touch, but then, if it had it, this wouldn't be A House of a Guy's Own. Ted Kaczynski was wrong about a lot of things, but not about having his own place.

Something there is in a man that longs for the time when he could hear himself think and she couldn't. When he could say to himself, "Let me buy you a cup of coffee, Mike," pull a can of corn with a spoon already in it out of the refrigerator for lunch, play Steely Dan indiscriminately, and maintain a filthy toilet without anybody being appalled. A place where, by virtue of there being no roost, he ruled.

For a while I had seen it as a trailer in the back yard behind the basketball hoop, attached to the house by the merest wisp of a phone line, or maybe not. But the gravitational pull of the mother ship

3

would soon pull it into lower and lower orbit until it would be captured and refitted as a play house. The same held true for the much-to-be-dreaded addition, where, after having your life torn open and exposed to carpenters and the elements for six months to two years, you end up still well within earshot of "Oops, I Did It Again" and they have but to fling open a door to wail, "Mom won't let me have a [bag of] caramel[s]!"

Then, three falls ago, alarmingly (and, I thought, fatally) ill with an undiagnosed something that caused shooting pains where the heart is generally thought to be, I had just returned from a second fruitless trip to the ER when I noticed, on the floor next to me, an info sheet on a little house for sale a few blocks away that my wife had brought home to show to a friend. In my delusional state (and thinking it was another house entirely), I bid on it. When I came to, I was the owner of a hundred-year-old farmhouse/student slum, just out of reach of the children's current bicycle range (although I may have to move soon). Once we closed, it was furnished within a matter of hours with all the things from former lifetimes that my wife would not have in the house: likenesses of me, my mother's lamps and tables, the secretary from my childhood bedroom, Arthur's bookcase, Uncle Max's flower pot, the samovar and candlesticks Dad got from the scrap metal people in lieu of payment, and even my old bachelor bed with the notches on the headboard, looking just like it did before it turned on me.

Since then, life has been good in the House of a Guy's Own despite little things, like snakes and vermin—no big deal; my firstborn is thriving, so it must not be biblical. The plagues resulted from not so much a defiance of Jehovah (although, Lord knows, I try) as of the fact that the HOGO could also be known as the Little House on the Landfill, sitting as it does at the foot of the sloping backyards of an upper crust of older houses whose owners never envisioned a human habitat springing up on their refuse or they might've thrown out a better class of garbage over the years. The landfill of a hundred years ago has grandfathered-in field mice that get cold in the winter and garter snakes that get hot in the summer and naturally want to come inside: for them this is A House of a Varmint's Own. Having escaped the scurrying of family members, I don't much cotton to (we're folksy here at the HOGO) watching rodents scoot past when I should be lost in reverie, or take any pleasure in prying their crushed bodies out of the traps or in grabbing one half of a snake while the other half squirms back behind the kickboard in the kitchen. The ones captured intact get to try out life on top of the hill, something they could only dream of before Mike Feldman. A nice feral tomcat on patrol would be ideal, but let in just one living thing and it opens the floodgates; besides, cats are higher-maintenance than mice, which at least know how to make do on their own.

The House of a Guy's Own provides refuge for other guys who don't have a house of their own, at least one free from beds they have made, and should really be tax deductible on that basis. Here guys can open up and say nothing at all. I get meter readers with a lot going on in their lives coming by, and plumbers who run deep if you give them a chance. In fact, it's getting so busy, I may need another place to go to. Now and then I confess to wanting to relocate lock, stock, and barrel to A House of a Guy's Own, and once or twice I even moved in a few pairs of pants. On one occasion, after thinking I had, in fact, vacated my family home, I waited around here for hours, and, when no one seemed to notice, I went home. Well, I was hungry—I keep limited food stocks (mostly gift packages, very seasonal) at the HOGO, and there's no cable or VCR so I won't get so comfortable I'll forget the obligations due three females, a dog, two gerbils, and a pair of Madagascar walking sticks. Should one move in, there (the middle-aged) one would be, living in the student pad of one's dreams conveniently located on the edge of pathos. Living with your childhood furniture after fifty is not a good sign, and, in fact, not very good furniture (they call it Depression for a reason); anyway, I was never good at living alone full time, tending, as I do, to face my mortality in lieu of light housework. Besides, if I lived here, where would I go?

A House of a Guy's Own doesn't work for everyone. Inspired by my example, a friend got a house of his own; while he was in it, his wife left him, leaving him with A House of a Guy's Own on his hands, and in a bad market. She, meanwhile, got a ranch house and a boyfriend of her own. Having a HOGO depends on having a stable household you're fleeing from, but not to the point of abandon. It can be pricey, but A House of a Guy's Own makes a great midlife present to yourself, which turns out to be affordable when you consider what they're getting for a Winnebago or a Crestliner with a big Merc on the back, and with tax advantages not found in most midlife crises. A cabin up north might work, but a cabin in the city is a *pied-à-terre,* and, as the French say, you can't beat that.

So, every morning, after making lunches for the girls and feeding Sugar, I drive the five blocks, put on a pot of coffee, read the *Times,* and do what a guy's gotta do, or not. Afterward, I go home.

2

A Walk on the Mild Side

Right off the bat, going out the door, a couple of little trees coming up through my hummingbird vines give me pause, so I get the clipper, snip the suckers, and, "take two," as I'm fond of saying to myself. Obviously a couple of season's growth on those babies, but between the allergies and the back I didn't tend to much this biennium, and I am the only natural enemy a lot of these weeds have. Now they must worship me: they have multiplied and become weedful. Around the front for a good look at the garden. Important to take a good look at the garden every so often, just to show whomever might be concerned that, despite appearances, you're still very much on top of the situation. Important to avoid that abandoned-property look. My baby's breath overhanging the sidewalk delights many a passerby forced to circumnavigate it. Aggressive, that baby's breath. I inherited the garden from the former owner, who had a plan that was never revealed unto me, and I've kind of lost any interest I might have had in breaking the code, although I'm looking forward to enjoying gardening and a zestful sex life well into my seventies.

Currently I'm not quite old enough or female enough to really enjoy being in a garden getting my ankles scratched by itchy things and pulling up some plants but not others. My kids pretty much take up all my nurturing. About ten tomato plants and a couple of hot peppers are about all I can nurture. I don't even know what half these flowers are, if, in fact, they are flowers; it seems to me the distinction is steeped in politics. There's where I should dig it up, but then I'd have to put something in the gaping hole, and that's a can of worms. Unfortunately, no caterpillars—Eddie next door won't ever stop asking unless I find him one. He says someone promised him one July 15th, but I've seen these deadlines come and go before. I keep meaning to stop at a bait shop for him, but they don't fish with caterpillars, do they? Grubs or wax worms are not going to cut it with Eddie. You don't even see caterpillars anymore, I guess for the same reason you don't see butterflies. Possibly, Eddie's getting to them first; he's surprisingly quick with that jar. I did find him a snake in the garden last year, but he didn't like it at all. It wasn't a caterpillar, I'll grant you that.

Ambulance coming down the block—passed me by, this time. Holy Doppler effect. I wonder if Doppler had an *affect*, too. And what about the weather radar—was that his, too? What a guy. Ooh, the mail lady's sitting in her truck past the corner pretending to sort, really just hoping I'll come by. I'll go that way. Got to think of something to say, something not weather- or her shorts- (the gray with the stripes!) related, and not the old "passed me by again today!" non mot. Hard to say something original to a letter carrier; they've heard it all. Horn! A red bug driven by an irate upper-teens–low-twenties female nearly squooshed by an encroaching male counterpart in a white Campus Cars Corolla unabashed though she nearly was. "That was close," I quip to the mail lady. "Yeah, there's a lot of close ones around here," she says. She's wearing the large gold hoops she favors. I'd like to get her some for Christmas, but I don't want her to feel funny every time she doesn't bring me mail, or to think that they mean anything other than, on some level, I think we're meant to be. "I think they deserve each other," I say. She laughs. There's a bruise on her thigh. Probably nothing.

Going this way has the advantage of missing the Toyota with the handmade bumper sticker, "This Car Gets 35 MPG—What Are YOU Doing for Homeland Security?" I'm walking, that's what, pissant! Heard of it? Or are you too busy whizzing past terror suspects video-taping the capitol in broad daylight? Again I entertain, but reject, the notion of wiping my ass on the bumper sticker. Don't want to set a precedent. It's just the neighborhood; another bumper says, "I will be a postfeminist when we live in a postpatriarchal society." A bit wordy when it could just say "Fuck Men," although that might send the wrong message. Well, you know what they say: "wild wymin never get the blues." Just up the block they've buried a cement deer up to its belly—must be a deterrent. If you were going to steal a ce-ment deer, and that's a big if, you'd probably pick one you didn't have to dig up first. I had noticed it was on its side all winter, but I thought it was just feeling poorly. First sign of spring when people put their cement deer in. I feel like I'm walking funny today—either these pants don't have a lot of give or they've just taken enough. My gait is off its hinge . . . feel like I'm pulling to the right, running on the rims. For seeing the mail lady, I now have to head through the park, via either zoo or playground. Not the zoo. It's like a zoo in there. All these kids in plastic animal masks the tapirs have been known to swat off with twenty-foot urine sprays. And that's before it tapers. Playground, then, trying not to look like a child molester on his lunch break, but, God, with these stressed khakis, oversized iguana tee shirt (a birthday present from the Virgin Islands), and ratty old gray Mephistos with the unintentionally lavender laces I dyed with wine (the tea made them too brown), I look every bit the guy everyone makes a point to observe in case they should be asked.

Plus my Mariners cap is still pristine, which is so *not* me, so anti–big government in its neatness.

A kiddie birthday party in the park. Adults drinking beer while their kids pound each other with plastic bats—we must be in America. Wow, nice to have kids who'll still play with you. I begged Nora to go to the park yesterday, just for old time's sake. I told her, "Basketball—tether ball—two square—name your poison. We'll throw rocks in a bucket filled with water, so they'll splash. Anything." About two episodes of *Boy Meets World* later, she came outside where I was reading the paper. "You're ready, then? If so, to do what?" I asked her. "Throw rocks in a bucket of water—isn't that what you said?" So we did, and it was well worth it. What am I going to do when she no longer wants to throw rocks in a bucket of water? What have I got, a year? Six months? The mommy by the old-lady-in-the-shoe slide just gave me the evil eye; I knew it. Well, time to tramp down to the lagoon for the daily scum clarity and color check, anyway: thick, foamy, a greenish mocha. Something flopping around in there, and I don't blame it. Could herald the start of carp-mating season. All that thrashing about must attract the female, at least at first. After a while, I bet she's repulsed by it. I bet she doesn't care if she never sees thrashing again. Occasionally you see a muskrat in the sludge who must think he's died and gone to heaven. A muck-rat. Canada geese make me run the gauntlet (those aren't cigar ashes all over the park, mister), taking me entirely for granted as not being any kind of threat. I hate it when geese act like women. Here's one that looks at me and mockingly honks twice, one for "lo" and one for "ser." They used to at least hiss, but times change, waterfowl change. They even used to leave, but now they just sleep on grates downtown over the winter and honk for change. Looking out from the bridge, lime carrageen bank to bank, and just starting to set up: a Jello salad for giant Lutherans. The weed harvester is back for more Sisyphean duty. Hard not to see symbolism in the weed harvester, but I try. Seems to be somebody-who-works-for-the-city's niece's best summer job ever, and I'll be darned if she doesn't look pretty cute atop it, jerking those gears and levers back and forth to keep the kelp stream steady and true.

No Mexican gentlemen enjoying a barbecue today. Cinco de Mayo took a lot out of 'em. Maybe they're all cooked out. You need some time away from the park. The lake looks different without a Mexican polka soundtrack, though, more norte Americano. Time to stare across the lake and go back 200 years in time, maybe 254 (to subtract me, as well), although I can never quite remove myself from the picture. If you stand just right, you can crop the disturbingly crematoriumlike St. Mary's Hospital stacks from the scene and see what the lake used to look like before the coming of the Catholics. Windsurfers aren't out yet, the wusses. They've got wet suits, big ugly Day-Glo ones, so what's the problem? My brother Arthur windsurfed so much he popped a ganglion, which looks like one of those creatures in *Alien* struggling to emerge from his chest. Windsurfing, sail boarding, whatever, either way it makes no sense, what with the invention of the mast. The bass boys don't hold their Mercs in the water. They're no fools, except for bass fishing. This lake gets a cheeky little wind out of the west that blows inland a good 1,500 feet. All right, so it's little. But, walking around the rim most days, you have to hold onto your hat while people driving by, sealed in their Tauri, think you're nuts; why don't they got out and face the music? Like people who park at a lake. Never get out of the car, doing God knows what, smoking, listening to Rush Limbaugh. Usually at this point I would walk the beach along the water line, but today the new crop of lifeguards is being trained. No offense, but it looks like they had to relax the weight limits to attract candidates; it must be hard getting kids to lifeguard when it's so much easier to make party drugs in your bathtub. They have to swim out with pontoons around their necks and drag somebody in—hopefully it's a mark and not some unfortunate wader—to the beach. The capo is shouting, "No life signs! What do you do?" "Throw 'em back in!" I want to say but don't, because some day that could be me lifeless on the sand with only an overweight girl between me and life as I know it.

The Old Man and the Winnebago's Winnebago is here; some dope in an SUV has him parked in. Good thing he won't be moving it until September. The W's faded just about into invisibility; the Plexiglas, thought at first to have been a quick fix, seems to be holding for yet another season, obscuring the driver's view to his left, and a new opening has been patched on the fuselage; possibly a vent or some other unnecessary doodad has been taken out. No sign of wife. She might have passed on down south—she looked older than him and he's no spring chicken. Her Mao T-shirt's still stretched over the back of the passenger seat, maybe in tribute. I always mean to talk to the OM and the W, but he seems to not enjoy eye contact should you happen to pass him out filling his water jug. Perhaps he's been hurt. I'd ask him if it was already hot down there and work around to the fate of the Old Woman. This leg of the jaunt uses the rutted jogging path where the rule of the road is "I yield." Some of these guys come steaming down the gravel like they're in training for the last days of Pompeii. One was jogging with a cell phone the other day—that has to be counterproductive. If he clutches his arms and goes down, hopefully it won't be the one he dials with. Occasionally a biker comes close enough to stir the hairs on your nape, if your nape is what I think it is. No one around here says, "On your left," although the other day a lady, badly out of breath, did gasp, "On your right . . . I mean on your left," leaving me so confused me I two-stepped down the incline and was nearly dashed on the plastic cups and tampon applicators. Amateurs. The pros in Chicago clamp a whistle in their teeth that they blow as they brush you back.

The howler monkey is howling. There's a shocker. Why they put howler monkeys in a residential zoo I don't know. I ought to complain, but I don't want to make a big whoop-whoop-whoop about it. These howlers are very insecure, even for monkeys. They need constant reassurance and apparently never get it. Yeah, well, you don't hear much of a peep out of me. The lion already wakes me up when he's having a bad dream, perhaps the one where he's trapped behind cyclone fences with a couple of mounds of dirt, a few denuded trees, and a female who's totally indifferent to him. Come to think of it, maybe that's my dream. Out of the park and into the Stop and Rob, where Nino, one of the few Hispanics from New Delhi, is ready with something from the news. Ever since he found out I was on the radio, he's been trying out material on me; unfortunately, a lot of the Karachi stuff I can't use. Today he tells me he was in J. C. Penney buying shirts, found two that he liked, and, noticing that one was made in India and the other in Pakistan, said, "I decided I'll buy the Indian one. The Pakistani shirt might explode!" I asked him if he was worried, what with SARS, about all the Chinese stuff—sparklers, nutty putty, light sticks, ceramic eagle statuettes— on the counter. "They've sat there for over a year, I don't worry about it," he says. A Tombstone pizza, the triple meat deluxe I'm always embarrassed to buy in front of him, and I'm back on the street past the house that flies the flag lighted at night, with its one remaining sign taped to it, the popular "Support Our Troops, Not Our Protestors." Methinks he protesteth protesthors too much. A lot of people in the 'hood are leaving their pro- or anti- (mostly anti- around here) war signs up on the lawn, rather than take them down and put them up again with every battle in the war on terror. Crossing the street to my block, I encounter a young woman who, smiling, comes to a very short stop to allow me to waddle past. She's done a good deed. Revivified, I sprint the remaining half block, pausing only in front for a good look at the garden. Everything's coming up, so I must be doing something right.

3

Feldman's Best Friend

I didn't have my first dog until I was twenty-one and married, too old for a dog and too young for a wife. We couldn't have major mammals when I was a kid because Clayton and Howie had had a collie before I was born and it came to an untimely end beneath an ice truck. This ban held even though the odds on a pet being crushed by an ice truck were greatly reduced and in fact nearly zero by the time I came along in all that postwar euphoria. The biggest thing we had was a guinea pig, Tony, which Arthur rescued from a research lab he was spending the summer as a youth-inizer; you could cuddle Tony or make him ride on the special boxcar Artie built for him on the Lionel line. He was great fun until we found him sprawled on the floor beneath his cage, having left what appeared to be a note scrawled in his sawdust; I think, like a prisoner released after too long in the slammer, he couldn't cope with life outside the pen. Other than Tony, there were just the lady bugs that came in under the window and that I tried threading leashes to and the usual ill-advised assortment of painted turtles from vacations and goldfish from fairs, and a salamander Arthur found while fishing that quickly went AWOL, turning up months later mummified under his slipper in the closet. We couldn't prove time of death to determine whether Arthur had actually stepped on him or whether the closet just seemed to the salamander like a cozy place to die.

But a boy needs a dog. I'm not sure about girls; mine seem pretty oblivious to theirs; Nora, while she's done a wonderful doggy memory book of photos and drawings, won't go so far as to walk him, and Ellie takes Sugar to the park only when she senses there are boys there at the end of their leashes. A dog helps train you. If you don't get a dog by a certain age, let's say eleven, you will never know how to scratch anyone behind the ear to give pleasure or get accustomed to having your commands ignored, and you certainly will never know the feeling of unconditional love. I can't remember the last time a female bounded up wagging her hinder in unmitigated joy as I cracked the door, unless it was on my way out. Cat lovers like to say this need for acceptance from something that will lick anything is what reveals dog people to be insecure and codependent, but Sugar and I just lift our legs to that. While I would sniff a butt under only the most carefully controlled conditions or lick my genitalia only if I could, something there is about the dog that speaks to the man. I enjoy peeing in the back yard under the stars with my dog; it's just unfortunate that the neighbors put in a picture window on that side of the house. I relate to the way he looks around self-consciously when taking a squat because I would, too, under those conditions. I might also eat until I vomit, although I would not, then, have seconds.

Perhaps I got too attached to my first dog, Rocky. I loved the way he had what looked like the outline of his head, ears up, in white on his gold chest, like an emblem. He was completely untrained, and I respected that. When we lived in the country, there was nothing he liked better than a good severed cow leg, which I found touching, even though I had to drive one farm down farther each morning to throw it in the culvert. I would say he could retrieve a cow leg from a two-mile radius; I'm sure with a little practice he could've brought home some better cuts, as well. While not quite at the human-interest newspaper article level, he had good disappearing/reappearing skills: once he slipped out of the car when we were on vacation in Alberta, only to show up later at the campsite on Highway 1. Back when wife 1 and I were running a day camp, Rocky once squeezed out of a cracked window in the Bel Air at a Kenosha mall (this dog could've been a cat burglar) on a Friday, ran off, and turned up at the first stop on my day camper bus pickup route, 52nd and 5th, the following Monday. Apparently he had bidness that lost weekend, like the time years later in Madison when he took off on the Fourth of July and was spotted alternating between two females in heat in Middleton quite a little ways away, despite the fact he had been neutered. Now that's pluck. I think I may have confused myself with Rocky at times, which is okay for a kid but probably not so good when you're thirty. When you live alone with a dog for a long time, differences seem to disappear, and it got so that the only difference, as far as I could tell, was that one of us enjoyed rolling on a carpet. True, he was high strung and a barker, but I've lived with a lot worse since. Rocky and I had ten wonderful years right up until he chased a rabbit across the path of a Blazer and, having lost a step or two by that age, failed to clear the grill (the driver came out yelling, "Is he all right? It's only a light truck!").

Sugar, of course, can never be my first dog, and that makes a difference, but I can see that many of the traits I thought were uniquely Rocky's—turning the head askance, for example, to feign understanding, very nearly forming the word "Out!", resting his head in my lap like I was the Buddha—are, in fact, dog traits, the very ones that have made us such a successful domesticated species. While Rocky was a mutt, Sugar has a pedigree, which puts him one up on me, but he doesn't flaunt it. He comes from hunting stock, his sire being Bodacious Black Gunstock; if I ever wanted to shoot ducks, he would be entirely in favor of it, since, so far, they have proven extremely difficult to swim out to and nab unwounded. Nothing incites him like a duck, unless it's a Pekinese. Hates small dogs. In fact, he's not much of a dog lover in general, considering himself to be a furry Feldman and not a yellow lab. At first I felt funny walking him because he looked like a gentile's dog, not a Jewish shepherd like Rocky, but, now that his whines and mine are pretty much indistinguishable, I feel he fits right in. I talk to Sugar, but I don't confide in him or depend on him emotionally as I did Rocky and the first wife, for that matter, but maybe that's just inevitable.

4

Gentile Like Me

I can imitate a gentile. Watch. Not bad, huh? Well, of course I've lived here all my life; by now I'm a Missouri Synod Jew. With the right lighting and an MGD in my mitt, I can pass. I've been told I do a very good gentile by guys who had to be told what a gentile was. (What good are gentiles if they don't know they are, anyway? And what's with the Mormons usurping the term? To a Mormon I'm a gentile, and they haven't even seen my act.)

Generally, I go gentile in situations where everyone else either is or should be: Super Bowl parties, traffic stops, taverns, sporting events, auto repair places, Farm and Fleet, during minor elective surgery or disasters (natural or manmade), while mingling with other Jews passing in the night for gentiles, or wherever coolness, aplomb, or just not caring all that much are called for. Did you ever know a Jew with a big cooler on wheels? I have a big cooler on wheels. Take the phrase "no problem." I can use it, although it is the very opposite of my two-word worldview ("Nothing works"). The fact is, everything for me is a problem. I even have a problem with my problems.

There is no point saying, "Got a problem with that?" to me. I do. A couple of years ago I had what I thought was a series of minor heart attacks, which resulted in my being rushed to the emergency room, twice. The first time, all wired up on the gurney, I was caught in the act of being myself and cried (well, it was the same room my daughter Nora had been born in, and irony makes me cry, especially when my impending death makes it possible). I noticed—believe me I noticed—the ER staff wouldn't even come around with a bedpan, because no one wants to be around that—an ax in the head, fine; a man blubbering, forget it. The second time, I corrected and went in as a gentile, Reagan-like, joking about my bum ticker (which turned out to be acid reflux) and got all the bedpans I needed, plus water, snacks, and the attentive ministering of attractive women in support hose.

Sometimes being a gentile means not saying much at all, not my natural bent. Volunteering "you got it," for example, when someone asks for something you don't particularly care if they get if it means you have to get it for them. "All the same to me," even when it isn't, is an evergreen, and of course the genial "I'll get this one." Watching old cowboy movies for additional dialogue can be instructive, cowboys being the ultimate gentiles, but you have to resist the temptation to push back the bill of your cap with your pistol finger while you say your piece or to twirl a lariat. Being helpful never hurts, "I could look at it for you" being the official mantra of the good-neighbor-Sam club and what makes gentiles so nice to have around, but you'd better have at least a working notion as to what it is you're looking at, particularly if there are moving belts or a husband who sometimes comes home for lunch. It's never a bad idea to be a gentile man with the ladies, and absolutely the only way to score with the Jewish ones.

My illusion is so real that more than once I've been mistaken for a guy from around here, even though I've lived here all my life (so why do they still think I'm from New York?). Convenience store clerks have been known to call me "Mike." I've been told this was very white of me and that was very Christian. I used to own a pickup. Three-quarter ton. Burly men in Oshkosh B'Goshes have asked me to pass them box wrenches and if I knew anything about two-stroke engines. ("They're tricky," I say.) I've learned to reply "wax worms" when asked what they're biting on, although I still don't know if that's a grub or one of those plastic lures that make you realize how stupid fish really are, and it's now second nature for me to reply "What you want to do . . ." when asked for directions.

Not bad for a kid who didn't even see his first gentile up close, except for the Prudential man, until he went to kindergarten.

5

Apologia pro Vita Herring

As someone who, for medical reasons, can't afford to be serious, I nevertheless appreciate how annoying this can be to others, even after producing a note from your brother, the doctor. What is a quality in me can often be a liability in the not-me, which might sound like self-loathing but really is just the hope of avoiding a pissing contest, especially these days. After all, I am a professional. I keep meaning to register my wit with Lloyd's of London; if I lose it at sea, I stand to make a fortune. Avoiding reality is my life's work—I was like this as a kid, back in the days when my name was Enough Already, and I'll be this way when calcified synapses make me appear to be quite amused at my non mots.

My type, by its nature, is anathema to some other types, many of whom are in positions of authority or think they are. Teachers either loved me or hated me or were somewhere in between regarding my early attempts to mock authority. Wives, secretly and not so secretly,

27

have at times wanted to gag me to prevent further installments of running gags at their expense. But fish gotta fly, birds gotta swim. There are biological imperatives here that undoubtedly have observable counterparts in nature, you know, genital displays among bonobos, practical jokes between magpies. I've had to put up with the congenitally literal, even to the extent of marrying one, but seldom bring it up, since these people have no sense of humor. My stream of unconsciousness may actually be how I feel, and therefore may be constitutionally protected, as a predisposition with its own genetic marker worthy of the respect accorded traits like alcoholism and red hair. Had we known about, say, ADD in my youth, I'd probably have been Ritalined out of the career I've had all theses years and be counting my days at the Motor Vehicle Department, State of Wisconsin. I don't know that I have any other dysfunctions that I might have made pay. As a serious individual I might have been more of a pillar of the community than I'm currently inclined to be, or of some service in some service organization, but I believe that other tendencies, like a strong sense of futility backed by an ambitious amount of lethargy, probably would've held me back. I've been to Rotary meetings, and my strengths did not come up under either old or new business.

Funny has its perks. Chicks like funny. Especially at first. Then, before you know it, the laughter turns hysterical. As with every performing art, there are "humor hags" who dig, hang with, and even make plaster casts of the penises of funny guys, but they've never cast me; they probably weigh in at about one-tenth avoirdupois the catch of even the lowliest bass player. Individuals not gifted in either light aside or pointed comeback may inordinately admire those who are, usually with the accolade "You're really quick," which is not necessarily true across the board. But, pity poor Pagliaccio—uneasy lies the head that wears the clown makeup. Who makes him laugh, besides, of course, the occasional dancing poodle? Sometimes you spend an entire lifetime defeating communication to discover you have no one to talk to, and, sadly, that's just fine with you.

Making little is a defense mechanism, but so is making much. Look at the earnest: what are they hiding? The fear that life is silly? Dealing with each and every thing must be exhausting; at the end of the day, I sleep like a baby, while the earnest are having dreams with alternate endings. There is something to be said for superficiality, particularly if it's surfaces you're trying to describe. Topography, after all, is a respected science. Beauty is only skin deep, but how much farther would you want to go? Subcutaneous beauty I can live without. Even the insightful and the empathic can get it all wrong, and the righteous be self-. And what about the stiff-necked: what is their problem, anyway?

6

Mad Mike

Ooh, people in cars drive me crazy. Thinking they can drive anywhere they want, and any way. Stinking parents of honor students. Volvos moving as if the drivers were girding their loins, smug in the knowledge they're cocooned and you're not. Minuscule women atop behemoth SUVs like abandoned brides on a three-tier wedding cake. Drivers who, if their other car is a bicycle, Harley, or quarter horse, ought to be astride it. Those with no business at the controls of any large piece of machinery, even without medication. The ones who couldn't manage two tons of mass at rest, and those for whom $f=ma$ means *force equals my ass*. Pedestrians-at-heart in way over their heads who would be much better off walking the three and a half miles on the shoulder except for the drivers like them who barrel down it. The bus-riding public too proud to admit it. Older drivers in Buick Regals on the prowl for a farmer's market or street party shortcut. Women who consider it rude to stare at the road while talking to someone on their cell phones. Camaros with blackout windows and a full-size Mexican flag decal where I would otherwise be in their blinking-light-trimmed rearview mirrors. Middle-aged bald guys, heads gleaming under the moon roofs of their cry-for-help blue Boxters. F-1-thousand-and-fifty super trucks on another plane of driving existence altogether, under-carriages embarrassingly exposed. Priuses with their high-bred owners righteously doing their part. Foc-me Focuses. Cadillacs with brown leather roofs, yellow bug screens, and horns on the hood heading for the ghetto rodeo with no wrangler visible in the saddle.

Car and driver: the double whammy. Cars would probably be all right on their own, but their drivers imbue them with their personalities, many of which are unsuited not only to traffic but to ambulation of any sort. Most would be just fine in land-based situations where, if you have to react in a tenth of a second, it's just to scratch your ass. Unless you're dating or working for them, people's unabashed selves are usually not your problem, but on the road there's no way around a series of rapid, unexpected, and ever-shifting relationships, over, hopefully, before they've had a chance to get off the ground. Could you hear the personal histories behind why they are unable to merge, yield, or anticipate, you'd undoubtedly be sympathetic, but out on the macadam there's just no opportunity, and very little ramp. Meet a second-guesser hesitating in life and it's merely annoying; on the two-lane you may not get a third guess. For the pent-up, driving's a release, the most fun you can have with your pants on without guns, except in Texas, where, they tell me, you can drive with a beer in your hand and a Magnum on the seat next to you, which at least sorts out the passive-aggressives from the real thing.

Lucky we can't in Wisconsin, because I've contracted road rage. The level of play has been ratcheted up several notches in our formerly sensible (if sluggish) rural/small town mix ever since cars started getting cockpits and autobahn suspensions and galloping horsepower returned. Even placid Mt. Horub has (four) mean streets (the chain-sawed trolls along the thoroughfares have taken such a beating they've had to haul them up the lawns away from the conflagration that was Main Street). You can't rise above it, and neither can I. I would probably like you if you weren't in a vehicle. Once you are, all bets are off. I wish I didn't, but I take everything you do personally, not just as affronts to common sense and the laws of physics. Ye who never signal, ye who never stop signaling. You rushing up to the four-way looking to tie, while neglecting to indicate that you're secretly turning and therefore lose by law and convention. You on my bumper, me on yours. You the technically within your rights doing the double nickel on our class-B highways because 55: it's the law. Those of you averaging 85 like you're actually in a hurry to get back to Minnesota; you the SOB in the Schaumburg Saab wending your way through the rustics. You, there, the Cutlass with real kitties suction-cupped to the windows. You up high in the gravel truck, which you must be surprised to find has anything left of the load by the time you get to the site. You, El Capitan, in your motor duplex with several generations of Larsons in it, some still breeding. You, kid, in the junker with the vanity plate "UNNSHRD." You, ma'am, in the well-maintained and garaged K-car, graciously yielding to any and all, your only fault being that you are ahead of me. You guys with the howitzer pipes. You in the International pickups with farm plates who appear to be tilling. You in the Caravan following a camel. You truckers playing cat and mouse, passing me from one to the other. You the right- and left-turn-challenged, who refuse to pull into the intersection to make your turn, knowing full well I am behind you and will not make the light, and what that obviously means to me, as well as you who pride yourself on weaving. You, the moped who knows his rights, even if you have, eventually, to be the mopped. The chemically intermittent, who come-to every few thousand feet before slipping back into your stupor. You who think your Jesus fish will save you, and you putting whatever passes for faith in Darwin. All of you.

I will eat your dust only so long; watch your mirror—I may be closer than I appear.

7

The Nondescript Charm
of the Bourgeoisie

I'm not a socialist; never was. If socialism means sharing a bathroom with six other people (a water closet socialist), I was a socialist growing up and hated it; if it means expecting other people to do their fair share as well as mine, I'm against it on principal. Am I a capitalist tool? I exploit only the ones I love; the rest, I pay cash. "Have I sold out?" is not the question; "shouldn't I have gotten more for it?" is. Yet the curse of the middle class hangs heavy upon me, the suburban white man's burden of being the luncheon meat in society's sandwich, suffering what Wallace Stevens called "the malady of the quotidian," measuring out our days in T. S. Eliot coffee spoons, now of course double pulls of espresso, maybe with a sprinkle of dark chocolate on it (the kind with the desirable flavonoids) on a special day. Just living the lifestyle as best one knows how, trying to raise children to think they are not privileged since that might suggest some gross inequalities inherent in what used to be known as the System these days when, if you want to question authority, you need to talk to yourself.

The late Harvey Goldberg, who *was* a socialist, and a brilliant and entertaining professor of history at the University of Wisconsin, was continually amused at my '80s faith in my generation of "baby boogies" to redress the evils of the American system as soon as we got into positions of power: "You're laboring under your misconception," he once told me after a discussion of the slow dawning of the Age of Aquarius in state government, the quiet revolution that's still not making much of a squeak. Be tough to man the barricades now, with this disc. Youthful rebellion and much-vaunted idealism aside (and then came the Dodge Rebellion!), hardly anybody really wanted to live in tiny enslaved Latvia, especially tiny enslaved Latvians. You can't really change a culture you're standing on (and, say, that's a nice Persian) without pulling the rug out from under yourself. The oppressed at least have something to gain. The struggle in America, after all, is to improve and not unimprove yourself. If your condition is already improved, there's always new and improved, so that you can supersize right to your cultural demographic's upper limit; the class ceiling. Not that you'd want to advance any further, even if you could, because that would be too unmistakable.

What is wrong with being middle class? Whatever was wrong with those Milwaukee German ladies with the geraniums on their always-swept stoops who were at their storm windows pounding as soon as you stepped on their lawns. The reflecting balls were there to enhance their worldview. I've hated geraniums ever since and am forced to admit I was actually glad when a virus knocked out most of them last season; small of me, I know, but very middle class. Blacks have at long last entered the middle class in Milwaukee, moving all the way up Center Street to the doorstep of Wauwatosa; now old black ladies are knocking at the windows on my block, but it still is a separate middle class with its own suburbs, like a separate heaven, to aspire to.

Ever since I discovered I was bourgeois, I've had reservations about myself, admittedly, a very middle-class thing to have. I mean, if the French have a name for it, it must be bad. We were, unbeknownst to us, petit bourgeois growing up (Dad having put together enough bad years for a good couple of decades), but now, son of, we're pretty clearly midi- or supramidi-bourgeois and qualify for a Citroën station wagon. My brother Dr. Clayton A. always told his kids they were "affluent" but not "rich," partly because he wanted to encourage them to fend for themselves and not to fend for his, and partly because he had high expectations for the fabulously wealthy. We were pretty much "God bless the child that's got his own" on 58th Street, since it seemed that Dad's ever having any to get was problematic. I found myself using the "affluent" thing, recently, when Ellie, who has a stable of what I would call rich (since they're not us) young friends, wanted to know how we stacked up:

"Dad." (She always uses the declarative, something inherited maternally.) "We're rich."

"First I've heard of it."

"We are. We've got tons of money. I saw your bank book."

"We're doing okay, subject to change. We're not Richie Rich. We're certainly not super-rich, which is the new rich."

"We have a lot of money."

"They had bushel baskets full in Germany. Needed it for a loaf of bread. What time is your hair appointment?"

She was getting highlights to better fit in with her set, all of whom seemed to be named Larson. But it illustrates something (doesn't it?)—if nothing else than that I'm embarrassed to be doing well when others aren't and that any such embarrassment is foreign to my eldest, who seems to measure her days in fashion statements. I may have failed her in not giving her more of a polemic to fall back on—if not a Marxist critique, perhaps a nonmaterialist prototype that, if nothing else, would save her huge amounts in dry cleaning.

8

Italian Vacation

I'm taking an Italian vacation this summer—not to Italy, but *come un italiano,* or at least like one of the several million who kennel the dog, stop the mail, pull the drapes shut, and hunker down for two weeks, or three if their itinerary is ambitious, in the cellar. (Where should they go? They're already in Italy.) *Il Messaggero* reports that a third of the roughly 20 percent of the population who can't afford a vacation once their hundreds of thousands of lire turn out to be 200 euros or who, for personal or health reasons, are not up to a trip, instead buy a sun lamp, garage the Lancia, take the plants to the neighbors, and fake *una vacanza* at home. Many spend the down time studying highlights of the destinations they are supposedly visiting and buying souvenirs over the Internet for show-and-tell upon their virtual return.

This seems to be a peculiarly Italian phenomenon, or maybe they just can't find a spot on the beach, what with the Germans taking up large portions of Italian sand (if we are to believe Prime Minister Berlusconi); the French don't seem to be in France in August, while every ambulatory Brit heads for Spain, hoping, perhaps, to bend one with Beckham. The psychologist Maximum Lattanzi speaks of the Italian "holiday mole *[vacanzieri talpa]* paralyzed in the presence of a huge inner emptiness" upon finding no one in his address book to go on holiday with, suggesting that certain individuals who believe they are islands seldom visit them. Signor Lattanzi is a member of an organization called Help Me, which intervenes with those barricaded in their homes watching Formula 1 racing for fourteen days straight rather than say *"in nessun posto"* when asked where they're going this year.

Having tried for years to get one of my (three) friends, Henry, Herb, or John, to go with me to Europe (Italy, in fact, right after Amsterdam for a little window shopping in the red-light district) to no avail (if I go again with my wife, the NATO alliance will suffer—last time Sandy had a French Laundromat owner, summoned from her home, throw a fistful of francs Sandy had mistakenly fed into a washing machine *à sa tête*), I know how the holiday mole feels in his hole; in fact, I may be a New World variety. I could travel alone, but for me a vacation is getting away from myself—impossible under those conditions; if the family can't or won't (or both: we don't so much travel as take our act on the road), you don't have a lot of options. Fortunately, given my schedule, it's pretty hard to tell whether I'm on vacation or not, so I simply stop reading the paper, shaving, or wearing socks and hole up watching television for women (once again, a departure) and, of course, the travel channel, which just broadcast an excellent piece on how to haggle for a sea bass on the wharf in Tokyo (hint: go late in the day, but not so late that the ice has melted). I don't really pretend to have traveled, but I emerge so broadened, people assume I have.

II

Breeding in Captivity

9

Leave No Parent Behind

I'm a parent; I guess that's apparent. My girls—Zoloft and Prozac—are my antidepressants, although recently Zoloft has stopped working. I love having girls, but I do bemoan the fact that I'll never have the chance to show someone how to pee in the toilet, like my dad showed me, by trying to sink his Marlboro butts. (Hit 'em in the filters, they won't go down.) Being the youngest of four boys, and never having had the advantage of a sister, I thought what a wonderful opportunity having girls would be to learn about females from the ground up. All I've learned so far is that they're female from the ground up and from the get-go, and if you don't want to get hurt you'd better get out of their way.

It would be too easy and too accurate to say that the eldest, Ellie, is a knockoff of her mother. I may not even have been involved in this one; I don't recall any activity in 1990, and her uncle (who, minus the five o'clock shadow, they're both ringers for) does show what some would think an inordinate interest. Most likely Sandy did it with a home cloning kit. Ellie's a great kid—I love her spunk—but she doesn't tolerate much in the way of fathering, sensing instinctively that an artifact has no natural rights. If nothing else, Ellie's lack of identification with me proves that her mother's identical attitude is genetic. I once asked Ellie—we call her Truman because she has a tendency to drop the big one—to quiet down, and she said, "You yell! Mom yells! It's in my genes!" Now I just let her express her inheritance and pretend I have to finish something in the basement, when I don't even have a workshop in the basement anymore. The little one, Nora, is more like me, although she still votes with the majority (has to or she'll lose her credentials). Organized soccer holds no appeal for her, whereas Ellie's soccer schedule runs three pages on the refrigerator any given season, and she keeps moving up—now she's in the tricounty league, next it'll be the tristate, and eventually they'll be playing Venezuela for the cup. (All this for a sport no American kid has ever made a dollar at. What kind of sport doesn't let you use your hands, anyway, but encourages you to hit a large leather ball with your head? The Mayans at least played with human heads, which made the game interesting.) Anyway, Nora, like her dad, is not a joiner. We discovered that right after paying the $2,000 nonrefundable Karate America tuition. You know, so you can wear the blue outfit with your name on the tunic to the mall. At least she's stopped leaping at me yelling *"i-yah!!!"* She prefers things that don't require others to be present—writing, reading, drawing, videotaping the dog, working on dance routines, and so on. Believes in the one-good-friend theory, whereas Ellie needs ten or twelve in rotation and is already mixing and matching for the inevitable sorority.

Being a father is pretty much a cakewalk, since nobody expects much of you. When they were little, I tried to elbow my way into the day-to-day, hands-on parenting, but after being stung a couple of hundred times, I learned to keep my distance. Women may say they want you to be involved in child rearing, but it's not that end of the rearing they mean. If you're up for a challenge, try cracking the circle of mommies at the next play group—they clam up, and some even jump up on the kitchen chairs and clutch their cargo pants, whereas moments before they were comparing stretch marks like battle scars. I would have been happy to show mine, and, believe me, I have them. Don't get me wrong, I love having kids. It's what you have to do to get them that gets to me; thanks to technology, a woman can have a child without a man, but how's a man going to have one without a woman? Rent a womb? Someday, perhaps, a breakthrough male will carry a child in his otherwise uselessly enlarged prostate, but I sure hope it won't be mine. I think a guy could do it in a lot fewer than nine months, though, if he had the right tools and the weather held.

I am an older parent. And older. I didn't decide to have kids until I was in my forties. Actually, I never decided, but that's another story—I was told, eventually, and then only on a need-to-know basis. My only clue were the dates circled on the kitchen calendar in red marker, with the enigmatic notations that I now know were temperature readings of something. At the time I just thought she was keeping an almanac. At least with Nora I was told, "I need some sperm on Friday," which, hyphenated, was her working title. I was forty-four when the second one was born; by the time the girls are all grown up, schooled, grad-schooled, married, and divorced, move back in, go back to school to retool, and finally leave again, I'll be seventy-four, and finally, hen willing, an empty nester with my whole life ahead of me, or at least a good eighteen months. On the other hand, maybe, like their mother, the girls will never leave—what then? Friends who skipped the '70s and got right down to it are already on their second or third family or have raised their children as close to maturity as is currently possible and are free and clear somewhere in the Lombardy region of Italy. They may have missed the free-love decade, but it wasn't free, and it wasn't love, anyway.

In a way, I was meant to be a father, even though I personally didn't mean to—it's a damn shame some feminist revisionist psychotherapist of the near future is going to ruin it all in retrospect. I tell my girls (1) remember how nice I've been to you in case somebody tries to tell you I wasn't, and (2) look (pulling the tufts)—I have hair! A man tends to live for his kids because he knows his wife's just waiting him out for those thirteen years alone she's entitled to according to actuarial tables, and with the million bucks paid out from the policy she was prescient enough to take out. Overall, though, midlife is a good time to have kids, really—if you're lucky your midlife and their adolescence crises will occur simultaneously and your ships may pass within sight of each other in the night in similar straits; flares should be kept onboard for just that eventuality.

You do worry about whose responsibility you will turn out to be should you unexpectedly survive—if it's Ellie's, I'm in trouble. After all, she's the one who got so mad at me when she was six or seven that she said, "Dad, when you're dead, I'm going to bury you in the backyard in a cardboard box, and every morning I'm going to poop where your head is." This my punishment for teasing her about a boy. She's calmed down slightly (or it may just be that I try to stay out of her face), but, still, hers is not the kind of attitude you'd care to associate with power of attorney, or hands on the wheelchair near bodies of water (and we're on an isthmus). Even Nora, a sympathist, told me, "Dad, I play a lot with you now—when you get old, it's Ellie's turn."

10

Runaway

Ellie was stuffing a few things into her backpack—a little toy baby carriage, a couple of books, her Big Bird radio (which she never listened to prior to leaving home), her diaries (just names, no details, since she can't spell them), the board with magnetic shapes she hasn't played with in years, her watch with the crayon hands (which she can't read yet, or she'd know it was too late for this)—and sobbing. "I'm running away! For real! I know how to open the door—you can't stop me!"

I realized she was right. Once you can open the door, that's pretty much the ballgame. All the trouble I've ever gotten into came as a result of opening a door. But when you're six, where do you go? Stay with little friends? Motel 6?

"Where are you going to go?"

"Around the block. I don't care, anywhere. I hate it here. You always make me share, and you never make Nora share because I'm the oldest."

"Honey, I'm the oldest."

"Kid!" she screamed.

"Nora shares," I said. "She's really good about the 'one-day rule.'" The one-day rule is one of those face-saving laws parents bend around their child's already habitual behavior, in this case the fact that something new is new only for a day and, the morning after, of so little interest that no one cares where it is or who claims it. Ellie has a quite aggressive notion of "sharing" that consists yanking whatever it is out of her sister's hands while saying, "You've got to learn to share." As far as I know, she has never thrust an object into her sister's hands and said, "Here! I have to learn to share!" which, I'm sure she'd say, is because she already knows how.

"Will you help me pack?" Ellie asked, frustrated at not being able to make enough of her life portable.

"Sure," I said. "In fact, you can have my old suitcase."

"You don't need it?"

"Nah. If I do, I'll give you a call."

"I won't have a phone."

"Right. Boy, that's going to be tough on you. Listen, feel free to use ours anytime. Here, look, you can put your blanky in here, essentials here, food over here. Beats tying it all in a tablecloth and slinging it over a pole like we did when I was a kid. I don't think even hobos ever really did that. Look, here's even a zippered pocket for your nookie. Let's get you a toothbrush, and a washcloth and soap—sometimes water pools up at the curb and you'll be able to wash up."

"You're kidding, right?"

"And, here, take my Bass Pro Shop hat to keep out of the elements—it looks better on you, anyway. Then, when you wear it, you'll think of me." She took the hat.

"I might go halfway around the block. Or maybe out in front of our house, down by the street."

"Whatever. Looks like rain though—you want to take a tarp?"

"Is there just someplace I could sleep here tonight?"

"I think we could work something out."

We spread out a pad and sleeping bag on the floor of the computer room, and Ellie took everything out from her bag and placed it around the perimeter.

"You'll be comfortable here?" She nodded. "You'll have privacy, and you can use the bathroom any time it's free. And you don't even have to see any of us you don't want to."

Ellie lay on her back on the sleeping bag with her hands behind her head. "I may sleep here tonight," she said, "and I may not."

11

Is This My Day On?

I've adopted the Nora Feldman approach to workload, a.k.a. "Is this my day on?" It seems just a few weeks ago (and, in fact, it was) that I introduced Nora, now three and a half ("three isn't a lot," she says, "but three and a half is"), to the concept of having a day off, which, after all, is made possible only by having, at some point, a day on. She took to it like a duck to water.

"Today is my day off. Tomorrow is my day off. The next day is my day off . . ."

"No, the next day is your day on, but it's only a half day. Then it's your half-day off. Then Thursday is your day off and Friday is your day on."

"I don't want to go on Friday."

"Well, maybe we can cut back a day. But then, after Friday you have a long weekend off until Wednesday." Which, somehow, usually turns out to be Fair Wages Day, or the Feast of the Holy Assumption, or some such, and she has the day off. She's one of the few Jews entitled to Catholic holidays.

As it happens, Nora has many more days off than days on; in fact, they call her into day care only on Wednesdays and Fridays or in advance of major holidays when they want to step up the production of plaster palm casts or whatever you can do with pipe cleaners, cotton balls, and empty Clorox bottles. Recycling in our community consists in giving the trash to preschoolers, who bring it home again, assembled. Ellie, the six-year-old, is particularly good at this, constructing battleships and office buildings that require the use of more rubbish than we in fact are able to produce, making us ultimately net postconsumer losers in trash, defying the laws of conservation by producing more than we consume. I honestly don't know what the neighbors think when we put out on the curb all those SnackWell boxes taped together, but it can't be good.

Since the work ethic skips generations, I've been pretty much able to adjust my schedule so that, theoretically, Nora and I have many of the same days off, but, since the work ethic does skip generations she's too busy for me, what with projects, lessons in Spanish, pre-dance, and proto-piano, birthday parties, meetings in parks, libraries, and espresso joints, running errands, getting shots, and generally leaving me alone with a house full of Barbies and only a few outfits I'm really tired of. Meanwhile, Ellie is off somewhere once again trying on another family. ("Some dads are a lot nicer, you know," she said to me the other day. "Yes," I said, "but you'll never have their noses.") Ellie is an important locus in a phone chain that prevents about a dozen to fifteen young girls from ever being out of one another's company for more than twelve hours over the course of the summer, additionally making it possible for her to sample what her life might have been like, ideally.

Nora still shows up for dinner, but I know it's just a matter of time, what with soccer practice, swimming, and tumbling just around the corner. And I've started going to work on my days off.

12

My Daughter Says Hello

This is how it starts. Well, not really. She liked (or even puppy-loved) Benjamin, but that all changed when he turned four and became more interested in having a big boy kick a soccer ball at his head than in jumping on Nora's back (her song "How can I stop him, he's so big?" dates from this period). Being three and three-quarters herself, Nora has been around the block once or twice—although not by herself—and knows there's a whole world out there beyond that day care door (or, as her six-year-old sister, Ellie, likes to point out whenever she's in a crowd, "there's a lot of people in the world").

Last week, Nora strapped on her sister's way-too-big hot-pink Barbie roller skates (which give her several inches both in height and in step) so that I could hold her up going down the big hill to the park, where, it happened, two boys of about ten passed us.

"That's what I call tall and handsome, " Nora said, meaning either one or the other or both. This hit me hard in two ways; one, I didn't want my little girl to get married and move away, and, two, Nora has told me she doesn't think I'm handsome, even though I told her little girls are supposed to think their fathers are "the most handsomest men in the whole world" no matter what they look like.

"You're not handsome," she says. "Shave here, shave here, grow this," touching in turn my left cheek and my right cheek and brushing my chin, "then maybe."

After the boys passed, Nora said, "They probably don't like my hair." Nora has a thicket of hair, which she occasionally tries to brush to get what she calls the "Rastas" out. She also believes she's chubby, which she is not, primarily because her sister, skinny as a rail, makes a point to use it in any reference, as in "Nora hit me with her chubby little hand!"

"That's still your baby fat," I told her.

"I'm no baby," she said. "What is your head thinking, mister?" (Besides her Krazy Kat syntax, she speaks with a kind of an accent, too. We spend a lot of time trying to pin it down: Romanian? Azerbaijani?)

"I have big cheeks," she said once. "I hate my big cheeks!"

"You have beautiful cheeks," I told her. "People love your cheeks. You have dimples in your cheeks!" Unwittingly, of course, I had insulted her, because she still confuses dimples with pimples. She really is a doll, but it's true, she and her sister, together and back-lit, look like the Trylon and the Perisphere at the 1939 New York World's Fair. I would wish neither of my daughters a body type, since without one you can't have body-type issues, but what can you do? I should have seen it coming this summer when proto-lanky Ellie began showing a preference for tank tops to accentuate her long lines, now extending well over four feet. I'm only grateful she's distracted by the specter of her baby teeth still not having all fallen out to pay much attention to anything else right now.

Meanwhile, back in the park with Nora, she had taken off the skates to run through the park in her white socks (even though I advised against it) and now wanted me to hoist her up and load her back into them for the uphill tow home, when, on the horizon, another pair of boys about the same ages as the first appeared.

"Hurry," Nora said, "they'll see I have little feet. Or maybe they'll think I'm just a little kid with big feet." We got her strapped in, and as I went into my lower-back-protecting crouch to get her rolling, she said, "It's all right to say hello?" in that way kids have of making what should be a question into a weak assertion.

"Sure," I said, "it's always nice to say hello," even though I'd prefer her to cultivate the "I-don't-even-know-you're-there" affect that has worked so well for so many of the females I've passed over the years.

"Dad," she said, "would you tell them hello?"

13

Nora Has a Problem

Nora has a problem. Nathan, the boy she loves to hate, likes her. "You know the worst thing? He follows me everywhere! At story time he scooches up next to me. He even danced with us at music time!" It's common knowledge she hates Nathan ("everything about him"), but his newly unrequited affection for her complicates her much-thought-out and revised "girls get the boys" plan, predicated on a swift and sure retaliation after one of the old unenamored Nathan's several trademark acts; tugging, scratching, and especially chasing girls. His reformation couldn't have come at a worse time; Nora had finally organized the girls ("I think I can get them to do it if I can get them to settle down") to plan a counterattack. The very next time Nathan chased a girl, Nora was to sound the command for the charge, and a phalanx of Bernie's preschool girls, Nora being the spearhead and Rebeca and Emma Rae the points, would rush him, trap him in the corner of the play apparatus, and put his hands through the steering wheel as he (and the others like him: Sam and Calvin, for instance) had done to countless girls. Nora, of course, refused to run,

56

instead flinging her sister Ellie's ironic "I'm *so* scared," at them, which, in nine out of ten cases, according to Ellie, works. There he would be pilloried in full preschool view on the wooden scaffold, and God help the boy who tried to save him.

She had to regroup. "I love that Nathan likes me," she said, accent on the "love." "I'll invite him over and tell him, 'I'd knock your brains out if you had any.' I don't think he'd even get it, though." She said she got the line from her mother, "who usually doesn't say things like that." Letting that go, I asked her if she thought that telling him she'd knock his brains out if he had any would make him stop liking her. "No," she said. "but at least I'd get to knock his brains out," showing the sucker punch that would do it, "if," she added "he had any."

14

Kinder, Not Gentler, Garten

Putting her aboard the white dot school bus (there's white dot, red dot, blue dot and one other dot), we feel like we're sending Nora off to the gulag or to the countryside where, on a collective farm, she will be disabused of her bourgeois ways and her beanie babies used for kindling, and just stare at each other in disbelief (not that that's unusual) after running alongside the bus waving "love" hand signs and wondering how we could do this to our sweet-headed little five-year-old. By the third day of kindergarten, she had thrown up ("at least you got that out of the way," I failed to reassure her), and by the middle of the second week, nosebleeds and "things that stick up and hurt" on her hands (blisters from the rings—just mastered!) had appeared. School was obviously a disease, and these were its symptoms.

She now had the schedule of a commodities broker. When she went just two half days and Friday at her old preschool (where they stressed communal vegetarianism, no preparation whatsoever for hot lunch), she used to stay up late with me, reading, talking, playing cards, what have you. Now she dragged herself to the couch at 3:30, too tired to do anything but watch reruns of *Brotherly* (formerly thought to be *Broccoli*) *Love,* all, as she put it, "because of a seven-hour day—*for a five-year-old!*"

Nor did she appear to be meeting many new people; Ellie, her socialite sister, came back from kindergarten the second day with the Franklin School directory and dialed her way through it. About 10 percent paid off in play dates, a good response for phone solicitation. Nora clung to the one girl she knew and had, in fact, rejected in less desperate times. Nora is not unsociable; she just prefers one good friend (with a couple of alternatives if the one is having a bad day) who agrees with her (usually agreeable) play terms (she will not, for example, tolerate all the girls being the mommy, knowing that too many mommies "ruin it"). Nora will never pledge a sorority (unless it's a service organization), while El is already picking out her outfits and accessorizing in proto–Tri Delt fashion. In this regard, Nora's the Feldman: she likes people, just not all at once, and not, for God's sake, every day.

"Why do I have to go to school?" was, fortunately, a question I've had forty-five years to think about: "Because in the old days, kids didn't go to school, they'd go to *work,* in horrible jobs in mines and factories, and make ten cents an hour."

"How much is that?"

"You mean a day?"

"Yes, how much?"

"Well, if you work a twelve-hour day, that's a dollar-twenty. But they probably hold some of that back for the meat pie they throw down the shaft at noon. And maybe they make you buy the rope they tie around your waist to lower you in. Maybe a dollar a day."

"A dollar every day? Some days could I get two dollars?"

15

The Guinness Method

After two years of study, a panel of reading experts commissioned by the National Research Council came down squarely between the phonics and "whole language" camps, calling for the "whatever works" approach that most of us as parents are already resigned to. Although I was raised phonetically (not Ebonically or Hebronically), and while I believe there must be phonemes in nature as surely as there were amino acids swimming in the primordial ooze, all I remember about my own early reading experience is that there were some kids who could read quietly to themselves and some who either couldn't or wouldn't. Sure, I remember "sounding out," and its limitations, particularly reading aloud to the class the word "photographer" as if it were, as it should have been, "photograph" with an "-er." There may be languages with a consistent set of rules, but English didn't seemed to be one of them.

My wife and I still try to talk phonetically to our kids, although they have no time for it: "Just tell me the word, dad!" I do it sparingly, but my wife, who believes we were put here to have and to impose learning experiences, will sound out entire conversations. To four-year-old Nora's question, "what spells p-h-g-t?" I will reply (having sounded it out) "fi-git," which she will transpose, with great delight, into "fidget!" I'm hoping this process will somehow be of use to her, as with the library of children's books she has already committed to memory. By about age three, both she and her sister, Ellie, had memorized entire books so that, should you dare to edit *Amelia Bedelia* (which could use it), they would stop you cold and make you reread it from page one. Nora is still in that stage; if she were one of the living books in *Fahrenheit 451,* she would be *Owen,* by Kevin Henkes, although she can also double on *Angelina, Ballerina, If You Give a Mouse a Cookie,* and several adventures of Madeline and Winnie the Pooh. Childhood literature is safe with her.

Ellie is in first grade now, where her teachers don't seem to cotton to phonics; while I know Ellie is context-sensitive, relying on a kid who won't hang up her coat to invent her own rules of spelling and syntax seems a lot for her to bite off (or at least to chew—I've seen her bite off a lot). I began to get alarmed when she brought home sentences that read "IPW MI DAD" ("I played with my dad"), "IWNT SWEME" ("I went swimming"), and "ISPLT" ("I stayed up late"), which the teacher would dutifully translate and affix a big "Yahoo!" sticker to with the comment "nice sentences." What was she learning? Telex addresses? Acronyms of World Health Organization field operations? I envisioned her filling out a college application "IWNTBTCHR" ("I want to be a teacher"). What if, God forbid, I were blinded and forced to dictate something Odyssey-like to her (TLMI MOOZ: "tell me, muse!")? I expressed my concern at a teacher's conference but was assured that spelling and reading "would come." (Stop me if you've heard that one before.) Actually, the only thing that kept me from falling in with the phonics crowd were some of the other bumper stickers on their cars.

Still, she and Nora could "read" a book upside down and closed with the lights off—that seemed to indicate some faculties were working that might eventually be used for the good of mankind, or at least those of us within shouting distance. Nora, reciting *Sheila Rae the Brave,* does it with feeling, expression, and nuance—in fact, much more than ever went into one of my readings to her. You'd think she'd lived it. Still, aside from acting, or, rather, including acting, it was hard to see how any good would come from this without a return to the basics. Then, one day, Ellie brought home a Henry and Mudge from the school library—the one where Henry tries to give Mudge a bath and ends up taking one—and I noticed that Ellie seemed to be looking at the text as she recited—in fact, lingering on the words. Naturally, I was impressed with how well she was faking reading, when I realized this was a book she hadn't seen before. She was figuring out the words, making judgment calls on context that were mostly right, was—dare I say it—sounding out the unfamiliar. She was reading.

A few nights later, Ellie crawled into my lap while I sat with a book and read aloud from *Angela's Ashes,* the part where young Frankie gets his first pint of Guinness. "What's a Guinness?" she asked. I'm afraid that early education has taken a turn.

16

My Religious Instruction

Nora was going to walk circles around me until I said I believed in God. I said uncle but that wasn't good enough. Finally I was forced to believe; she has from the get-go.

"I believe God is in everything—a little piece of him is in everything," she explained to me when I was forty-eight.

"Who made God, then?" I asked her with the natural curiosity of the middle-aged.

"The wind," she said.

"Was he born? Will he die?" I wondered.

"He never dies—he's a spirit, and spirits never die."

Never having acquired a consistent religious point of view (we went to an orthodox temple but ate anything we wanted) I really don't know where Nora's closely held religious stock comes from— sometimes it seems Christian, sometimes Animist, I don't know, Zoroastrian, maybe. Rosicrucian. Who knows what went on in that vegetarian preschool with the Rasta cook? Her mother is an atheist because of God's comparative underperformance, so that wasn't the source. She just seems to have intrinsic faith. Since I have my doubts about everything, I guess I would be an agnostic. Nora's sister, Ellie, believes if there is a God she will get a TV/VCR combo with cable for her room. She is always saying "Omigod!" but I don't think that's a profession of faith. While initially wanting to be Christian because Christmas was a better holiday, Ellie more recently would say "It's good to be Jewish," at least before Hebrew school threatened to impinge on her soccer time; then it was not good at all to be Jewish. But Nora was always more epistemological in her approach. "How did everything start? I think about it all the time." Her version of creation started with tiny little insects turning into plants and animals, "and sometimes dinosaurs," and, to my childish inquiry, "which came first, the chicken or the egg?" Nora held that "the dinosaur laid the egg which became the chicken," leaving Darwin plenty of wiggle room. Underlying it all, for Nora, a Supreme Being, whose existence she conclusively proved when I was a mere 51½: "I know there is a God. I proved it. You know how they say if you write God's name on a piece of paper, cross it out, and throw it away, he will die? I lost the back of one of my earrings, and I looked for it and looked for it, and I said to God, 'I'm going to look one more time and if I don't find it, I'm going to write your name on a piece of paper, cross it out, and throw it away.' And then I looked and I found it!"

The fact that her earring back had been on her sock the whole time proves, additionally, that God works in strange ways.

17

Sometimes a Great Ape

"You're the silverback" is, for my money, the best thing Ellie ever yelled at me, and she's yelled a lot of things. For this we send them to school? She wanted me to countermand one of her mother's pronouncements (even though when she nails them to the door they're official), just not my role here among this particular claque. I don't know how other primates feel, but they just don't pay me enough. In fact, they don't pay me at all. Besides, she knows full well (that's *full* well) all she has to do is work on her mother unrelentingly for half an hour (tough cases take an hour) and she's got yet another backpack, array of cute pants and tops (one of the first and, come to think of it, one of the last useful things the father of girls learns is to call shirts "tops"; makes you sound in the know for a moment), or whatever she has to have by close of business. To Have and Have Now: the Ellie Feldman story. If there is anyone with any doubts about whether, given everything, we still want, the answer is tell me about it. If I might launch into a brief "difference is" tirade: we wanted a lot when we were kids, but the difference is we never got it, or, when we did it was the wrong one Dad grabbed on his way home from work. When we got something, we appreciated it more than it strictly merited (I mean it was only a snorkel swim set from the five and dime) because the odds against it happening in the first place were formidable—it took an annual event or a graduation in those days, and not from grade school or junior high. High school or better. Even if you got something for finishing high school, it was a fountain pen or a watch—if you got a car you were unheard of. Bar Mitzvah booty, aside from the bonds, which you couldn't spend for seven years and three months, anyway, was mostly unusable (the talis, maybe), although I've kept the thesaurus Ben and Gussie Stein gave me all these years because you never know when you'll need another word for "thesaurus" ("storehouse" or "treasury of words"; "onomasticon [rare]"). To summarize, parents didn't take pictures, they didn't schlep us places, and they didn't ply us with things; that's how we were shaped into the outstanding human beings we are today and why nothing like us will ever come down the pike again in this expansionary cosmos. We knew how to be unhappy with the little we got. Clichés notwithstanding, of course you miss what you don't have, but a real wanting, other than for the girl I used to dream about serially, was wanting in me. Clothes? Mom brought them on the bus from Gimbel's; they were bad; we wore them.

"We're not lowland gorillas," I replied.

Ah, the silverback male. Long may he turn it. But pity the poor schlepper down the line, at the end of the second row, culling the odd elderly female for a charity coupling, teeth going, lousy with nits and no one to pick them, some silver, mostly in front, sleeping on the matted grass right out in the open as predator bait. He coulda been a contender—still could be if something happens to Sampson. Not the biggest, maybe, but possibly the brightest of this lot, a trait undervalued by lowland gorillas (for all their other documented good qualities), although appreciated by Jane Goodall when she still used to come around. But even she liked the big ones.

"We studied them in school—you're the head of the clan!" It struck me then that what Ellie has wanted all along is an action father, you know, a Michael Feldmanegger, which it would take to challenge her mother once her jaw is set. Maybe that's what her mother wanted, too, not that that's any of my business. Ellie did tell me once that she would raise her kids "more strictly" but didn't go into details that might have compromised her own situation at the time. Nora said she'd have more rules, but for her rules are really a way of documenting how good she is—I can't even get her to step on somebody's lawn (and I've tried, as a kind of rule-breaking therapy. No luck.).

As for taking your cues from nature, well, we're not the great apes. We just try to be best apes we can be.

| 8

Home Alone

I'm having a kids-at-school attack, and it's only 10 A.M. the first day of. Nora would, by now, just be entering her third hour of Nickelodeon, her second of *Sponge Bob* alone, while drawing the latest in her line of Flaming swimwear. She would be asking for a "plate" right about now, a number two, usually; that comes with bagel, buttered, with sides of olives, pickles, that thin dried beef rolled into tubes, fresh fruit in season, sauerkraut when available, and, until recently, string cheese, which she now shies away from due to lactose considerations, something her mother put into her head. A number one is the same without the bagel. We just added a number five the other day, a fried shrimp platter I'm pretty excited about, despite the oil burns. It's been well received.

But instead she's sitting at a desk somewhere (all right, I know where—her third grade classroom), organizing her supplies, wondering why she wanted to go back to school so badly, and trying not to think about her stomach. I was the same way: mine used to churn. Waves of missing Sheryl, the legendary second-grade teacher, the old school, wash over her. She'll be fine I told her; we all have Sheryls, we all miss them. Meanwhile, back at the empty nest, where even the dog seems listless with no kids refusing to walk him, I pine for my three chapters a day, where we'd sit together and read three chapters; she, *Goosebumps,* me, whatever's around, books, printed matter, circulars. I don't know how to describe the quietude: it was like there was no TV on. After she'd read, she'd eagerly update me: "Remember that skull in the locker? The one with the glowing eyes? Well, he gave it to Cliff, who started having bad luck, too . . ." Maybe we'd play a few quick games of speed, or as many as it takes me to win. On to the Sims, where she is an in-demand contractor, specializing in trophy homes with every appliance, wall covering, specialty room, pool, and landscaping habitat known to the electronic arts (paid for by the "rosebud" cheat, but, hey, that's the construction business). Nora's Sim people don't move much (and she gave up trying to have babies because they were too much trouble once you had them), but her building supplies fly out of the bins.

Once, every twenty minutes or so, I try to get her to do something with me, anything, you know, outside—and, no, agreeing to sit with me on the porch for ten minutes doesn't count. "Nora—take a bike ride with me. It's good for my health," I plead. "It's not good for mine," she replies. "The seat hurts." "Maybe later?" say I. "Maybe not," says she. Basketball, two square, the beach, and the zoo also fail to excite, but she did invite me to jump into a puddle and waggle a rain dance with her the other day, and it was just what I (and, I suspect, the neighbors) needed. This is, after all, the same kid who, after going to the park with me once this summer (and, at that, to film a documentary), said, "Dad, don't get your hopes up—this is not going to happen again."

Ellie, the older one, would be, of course, up in her room with yet another friend whose name I can't recall (I now understand how Woody Allen's testimony was plausible), ordering in, making the occasional personal appearance to beg a ride or slip out to the pharmacy where—and here's a coincidence—James and Ben just happen to be hanging out (filling the quota of preteens allowed in at once). She actually pushes me out the door whenever she's on her IM, like I care what "snickerspuppy" has to say. She used to be my little pal—why, on my radio show, I carried her under one arm when I went into the audience and changed her diaper on the air. Now I'd be persona non grata if she'd take Latin. So that leaves Nora, or did, before compulsory education.

I'm sure I'll find ways of filling my time. Work, for example. I could work more than I do, but it's a pride thing. I could recreate; it's not impossible. "Leisure activities" doesn't have to be an oxymoron. My back's sore for only seven to ten days after I go to hit golf balls, and sensitive for another two, three weeks, tops. Everyone has a sport; mine is still in beta testing—when they roll it out, I'll be there, and with pads if necessary. I used to enjoy reading but don't much like to do it by myself any more. What's the point if there's no one to tell you what's going on in her book? For now, all I really want to do is kill time until 3:45, when the school verdict—"poopy" or "good"—comes in, and fix her and the friend she's brought home snack plates. I'm thinking of a pair of fours, with mandarin oranges.

19

Jews Close Lower in Light Trading

I'm glad Mom wasn't around to clip and send "Jewish Population Decreases" to me, although, in her honor, I scissored it out of the National page myself. The news would have been a stab in the heart, even though she would've felt vindicated that her polemics against mixed marriage and what it brings have been borne out. That there are Unitarian Universalist mothers, somewhere, sending this clipping out to their boys away at college, along with an upbeat note and possibly a few dollars, would have been little consolation.

"They will turn on you," my mother used to say, "and they'll raise the kids Catholic," no matter if they're Missouri Synod Lutheran, because "they make you sign a paper." Forget that religious dissent never reared its redhead with my first wife, a German Methodist, and erupted frequently, along with everything else, with number two, a 100 percent dyed-in-the-wool; my mother stood fast with the many of her time who thought that "marrying outside"

76

would finish what Hitler began, and that the war at home in Milwaukee, capitol of Baden-Baden, would have been fought for naught. They're gold diggers, and changelings. Marrying a *shiksa,* Mom said, would be like buying a pig in a poke, except that she could tell us what we'd be getting. As a consequence, my three brothers all married Jewish, but their male children all have married or are dating Asian women: what happens to a dream deferred.

Nationally, we're down 5 percent to a little over 5 million, when there used to be that many in New York alone. Once our Yiddisher forefathers forged their way into the hinterland and discovered that German girls in this country were amenable, the die was cast, if, indeed the mold was not broken. *Portnoy's Complaint* sounded the alarm, although at the time we mistakenly thought it to be about sex and not about gaining entrée from below; Eddie Fisher, who had just been forgiven for marrying Debbie Reynolds (she was, after all, Debbie Reynolds) muddied the waters by dumping America's sweetheart for Liz, and not because she was Jewish; a second cousin from California had gone over to the other side entirely and was living for all intents and purposes like a *goy.* "His father won't talk to him," she said, well aware that no amount of not talking would change things, "and his mother won't have them in the house when the father is there."

Mother, herself, adjusted pretty well to the unthinkable, only pressing for Wife No. 1 to convert, conceive and raise the kids pareve when I wasn't around to overhear. We failed for all the right, not the religious, reasons, and after a lazy rebound over a decade or so, after I mistakenly concluded that I had been avoiding Jewish girls like the plague all those years for nothing, I married one and (two lovely girls aside—a big aside) have had nothing but *tsoris,* albeit sanctioned *tsoris.* My wife, who herself had been avoiding Jewish boys for most of that time, would tell you she agrees. I don't know if we have heaven, so I don't know where Jewish matches might be made, but ours came from the bureau where resignation is finally issued.

Years ago, I had the notion of raising our girls as Christian (Edge-wood College, a Catholic institution that keeps them cradle to grad school, is just two blocks away) so that, eventually, they would find Jewish boys attractive. Catechism can't be any worse than Hebrew school, and they might even show up for that. Only after they were safely signed, sealed, and delivered would we tell them the truth: that they didn't have to convert, they already were. Still, we wouldn't want them to be seen as Jews in denial after the long struggle we had to get off de Nile. I'm bracing myself for the worst—Ellie's friends, while very nice, all resemble Bund youth; she trades somewhat on being exotic. Too soon to say for Nora, who, just this morning, dropped her mother's and my hands abruptly on the walk to school; thinking it might be because of one of the three young men just then shoving each other across the street ahead of us, I asked if they were the reason, and she yelled, "ARE YOU KIDDING?—YUCCCH!!"

We should have been stricter with the kids in reinforcing cultural identity, but, frankly, we've seen what marrying in the faith can do. While purists would quarrel with it, I've given Nora and her sister the accommodating "I don't care who you marry, if you marry; just raise whatever comes from it Jewish." When they ask why, I tell them, because of the suffering we've done over the years, and their mother's and my hope that ours has not been in vain.

20

Don't Kazaa for Me, Argentina

"They arrested a twelve-year-old girl for using Kazaa," twelve-year-old Ellie said. "Should I take it off my computer?"

"You should be all right—they just charged her parents. Only $175,000 an offense—how many songs you got?"

"A hundred and sixty. Some of my friends have a thousand."

"A hundred and sixty times $175,000 that's all. Does not compute. But there's an amnesty if you delete all your songs now, say you're sorry, and promise to go straight. They just make you join Columbia House."

"What? Dad. Can they see what's on your computer?"

"Yeah, I guess so." (Thinking what's on his computer.) "They must. But they're only going after the big offenders, like your friends."

"Everybody's talking about it [on IM]."

"Cool. We should go out and buy some bad music every so often.

Then I think it's okay—you're just sampling with intent to buy, legally speaking."

"What about you? You download a lot of stuff."

"For a while there I was. But now I'm thinking about buying the whole Tiger Woods thing, not just the back nine at Pebble Beach. Pebble Beach is nice, but you get tired of it. If I run into something I like, I go out and buy the program, and it turns out to be useless and a waste of money. I'm not saying that justifies it." I did download my entire mental catalog of moldy goldy hits, "Town without Pity," "World without Love," "Walk Right Back," "Sleepwalking," Paul McCartney saying "s—t" on "Lady Madonna," the occasional fondly remembered gag tune like Spike Jones's "Der Fuehrer" or "The Banana Boat Song." Stan Freberg. The entire British invasion. Well, not the Hermits or the Dave Clark Five, but the Searchers, yes, the Troggs, yes. If they were British. Quite a bit of blues, R. L. Burnside, Bobby "Blue" Bland. The young Muddy. "Dandelion," where the Stones sing with the Beatles. Filled three discs, tops. It's not like you're ever going out and buying that stuff again. I already own some albums in three formats—what do they want from me?

"I'm going to take it off my computer."

"I think you're right, hon. You can always tape it off the radio."

21

A Death in the Family

"Why did you have to tell me?" moaned Nora. I don't know. I should have known she would take it hard. I thought she'd want to know. What do you tell a kid when a neighbor dies, especially a mother? Especially a giraffe.

There's our block, then the next block down, then the zoo. We and the animals are in the same ward. We've had our babies together, our kids have grown up side by side, our females are probably in synch with theirs; theirs just see a veterinarian, that's all. The lions can hear me growl in the middle of the night; instead of a rooster, in our urban zooscape howler monkeys try to whoop the rising sun back down. We visit the old orange orangutan with the beautiful hands as if he were an elderly uncle in a nursing home who's been slipping a little. When they shipped out the stump tail and rhesus monkeys en masse, we felt like some of us had been arbitrarily rounded up and deported, even though these poor souls were descendants of the university's primate lab (where research once proved that a one-armed rhesus can still swing, but if you cut off his tail, he's screwed. What they did to the stump tails, which had nothing to lose, God only knows.). We pray they went on to a better life at a primate Sun City and are not currently testing cosmetics, which, admittedly, they could have used (particularly, if you must know, on their behinds). When an uproar over the care and handling of the elephants (one African, one Indian that fate had thrown together) sent them packing their trunks, we nearly left with them, although none of us would be able to revert to the wild easily; as victims of captivity, it's amazing we've even been able to reproduce.

So when Savannah had a son a couple of years ago, it was a big deal, particularly since most of us, possibly due to something in our feed, had been producing females. Well, a giraffe is going to stand out no matter what. A little giraffe appears to be eight legs folded up under an already formidable neck (you've got to wonder how the delivery went, particularly without the benefit of Lamaze), which despite the description comes out adorable, if gangly in several dimensions, kind of like a stretch colt. You wouldn't think a little guy like that would ever be able to rise to the occasion, but he did, and it wasn't long before he was nearly as tall as his mom, and just short of being a ringer for his dad, Raymond, who, unusually for our neighborhood, did not seem to take a direct interest in the rearing end of things, probably just ruminating on the giraffe equivalent of the father's mantra, "one time, one kid." Raymond did show him the ropes, though, where to lope, how to discourage the turkey vultures, and what to look for in a crowd (zoo animals instinctively can spot the kid who's going to wing popcorn no matter what some stupid sign says). Savannah, of course, never left his side, although that was certainly influenced by the limits of their enclosure, which, sadly, also proved to be fatally close when they were frolicking last Friday when she suffered her head injury. Savannah needed a savannah, but they are few and far between in Dane County, and usually filled with rows of John Deeres. Nora and I had entered the contest to name her child, but for some reason they went with R. J. (Raymond Jr.?), instead of Sid, but still we felt like godparents, or maybe a godparent and a sister. Then this: there, with the Zor Shriners in their fezzes and the sweet Norwegian ladies whose families (probably by their request) submitted a much younger photograph, the head shot of dearly reticulated Savannah filling most of a column in the obituaries.

There was no service, just a simple defleshing of the carcass by dermistid beetles in the UW Zoology department, where Savannah's lovely bones will be catalogued and stored, even though many of us were hoping for a waiver from Resurrection Cemetery (where you no longer have to be Catholic, but it helps) so that we might catch up with her in the next world, this time, hopefully, on her turf.

22

Freaky Weeky

After watching one too many Disney Channel kid-coms where sisters exchange personalities or mothers wake up in horror realizing they are their own worse fear incarnate, their own daughters, until it dawns on them they can now work it (girl) for some of those cute boys who've been hanging around her, or, rather *her*, members of the Feldman family awoke one morning to find themselves transformed into one another. The father bounded out of bed as his nine-year-old, Nora, having awakened with an ache here and a tugging band of muscle across her upper back after what must have been a bad night because she's never had such trouble getting out of bed, shortly thereafter screams from the bathroom, having found that she is about to brush the yellow teeth of a fifty-four-year-old man, her father, and in the mouth that says not happy. The mother—let's call her Sandy, for argument's sake—has exchanged personalities with the dog, owing him a player to be named later and a sizable amount of cash, and is now a male yellow Labrador retriever named Sugar.

Only the twelve-year-old, Ellie, too stubborn to be anyone else, remains her own sweet self.

NORA (Dad): "God-DAMMIT! Killed my back doing a cartwheel, and landed on a FUCKING soccer shoe to boot! FUCK!!" (three times, fast, like a hen would say it).

ELLIE (Ellie): "MOM! DID YOU HEAR WHAT NORA SAID?"

Mom (Sugar): Gets excited, thinking she's(he's) going to get a walk. Sits to be good but can hardly hold still. Turns head side to side as if trying to understand. Whines a little, over and over.

SUGAR (Mom): "I've got a million things to do, I'm not taking you" is what he(she) thinks he(she) said, but it comes out "Woof," so much like a stereotypical dog might bark it that he(she) gets additionally pissed.

MOM (Sugar): Picks up soccer shoe with her teeth and begins to trot over to the shoe rack and growls, "I'm the only one who picks up, around here" and then trots back for the other shoe, drooling somewhat over it. "SLOBS!" she barks, clamping onto the shoe and shaking it back and forth and snarling.

ELLIE (Ellie): "DUDES! WHAT IS FRICKIN' GOING ON HERE?"

DAD (Nora): "Is that my necklace? That's my necklace! TAKE IT OFF!" and reaches for the necklace around Ellie's throat. Ellie recoils in terror.

ELLIE (Ellie): "YOU GOT TO LEARN TO SHARE. YOU NEVER SHARE!"

DAD (Nora): "That's not sharing that's taking! YOU GOT TO LEARN NOT TO TAKE!" Ellie, hurriedly while still lurching back from her crazed father, gets it over her head just in the nick of time. Dad (Nora) snatches it.

DAD (Nora): (after snatching) "OWEEE MY ELBOW!"

NORA (Dad): (from other room) "That's tennis elbow, honey, from throwing Sugar a stick. Sorry about that. Say, you know, this

Disney Channel's not too bad. Raven sure has gotten big. My oh my, she's gotten big."

DAD (Nora): "Dad, that's disgusting." Waves hands in front of Nora's (Dad's) eyes. "You are forbidden to watch my shows!"

NORA (Dad): "Who are you to forbid me to watch TV? How can I not watch it—it's on all the time. I wish you would watch the Discovery channel once in a while or, God forbid, turn it off!" Realizing that she(he) sounds exactly like her(his) father when she(he) was a girl(boy) and yet finding herself(himself) a nine-year-old girl, she(he) is stymied and unable to move or say anything. Fortunately, she(he) has felt this way before and knows it will pass.

SUGAR (Mom): "ELLIE, STAND UP STRAIGHT. YOU'RE DROPPING ONE SHOULDER. YOU WANT TO BE SHORT *AND* STOOPED? YOU WANT SCOLIOSIS?"

ELLIE (Ellie): "Get away, Sugar. MOM! (to Mom [Sugar]) YOU SAID YOU'D TAKE ME SHOPPING. I'VE BEEN WAITING A HALF AN HOUR!"

MOM (Sugar): Not liking the sound of that, flees to the other room and curls up at the foot of the stairs to be most in the way.

ELLIE (Ellie): "DUDE WHAT ARE YOU DOIN'?"

NORA (Dad): "Dude, what are you duding?"

DAD (Nora): "She calls everyone dude."

NORA (Dad): "What ever happened to dudette?"

DAD (Nora): "No one says that."

Ellie comes over to try to get Mom (Sugar) to get up from the base of the staircase, but she(he) looks very comfortable.

ELLIE: "MOM!! YOU'RE BEING A REAL BITCH!"

MOM (Sugar), lying on back, cycles legs up in air, as if to say, "A bitch I ain't!": "RRUPH!"

NORA (Dad): "Honey, don't yell at the dog."

Sugar (Mom) scrambles up on his(her) hind legs with front paws on Ellie's shoulders.

NORA (Dad): "I think Sugar's trying to tell you to stand up straight! Look at that! Hah! C'mere, boy, you're man's best friend, you know."
DAD (Nora): "Uh, Dad . . ."

Sugar (Mom) rushes at Nora (Dad), lowers his(her) shoulders, and barks repeatedly as if she(he) were a intruder.

NORA (Dad): "Down, boy! Has your mother been training you?"
DAD (Nora): "Dad, can you fix me a plate?"
NORA (Dad): "Maybe you should fix your own plate."
DAD (Nora): "I have to? But I can't reach the cabinets."
NORA (Dad): "You don't know how tall you've gotten. Just do a me a favor and don't stand on the counter. Okay, okay, I'll make it."
DAD (Nora): Thanks, dad.
NORA (Dad): "Hey, Nora?"
DAD (Nora): "What?"
Nora (Dad): "Love ya!"
DAD (Nora): "Love *you!*"
ELLIE (accepting that Sugar is her mother): "MOM. C'mon upstairs and be with me. YOU'RE NEVER WITH ME!" Mom bounds up the stairs after Ellie, delighted to be allowed into her room.
ELLIE: "Will you take me shopping later? I don't have any tops."

This goes on for another 140 or so total hours of family viewing, or about two weeks of back-to-back Cosby reruns, until whatever it was, perhaps the effects of a power surge in the cable, finally dissipates, and all revert to form. Everyone in the family feels a bit chastened by the experience except Ellie, who thinks about what advantage she might take the next time this happens.

23

Cassandra

God is a woman, and she just tries to do too much. That's why the world is the way it is, you know, with so many things left undone. She's doing a hundred things at once, while he (the husband you don't hear about) may not do all that much but he has been doing it six days a week for the celestial equivalent of a working lifetime, thus making many good works possible. And him with an unfunded mandate of his own.

On earth it shall be as it is in heaven. Try giving to an altruist, sometime: they won't take. They're too busy giving. An admirable quality, but can one give too much? I wouldn't know, but even God giveth with only one hand; if you're using both, you may be in over your head. There's always someone, me aside, who's needy, and a never-ending stream of support and encouragement to provide to complete strangers who didn't even know they had it coming. As a silent partner, you could be supporting a family of four in Guatemala who will never know of your largesse, thinking it's just some *gringa* with *un poco español* and *mucho dinero*. I believe we should do for others, but at this point I need an other to do for me. Has a fella got to be downtrodden to get a little attention around here? You know, people in the first and second worlds have feelings, too.

Someone has to put a good face on charity, but what can be off-putting in another (not so much in yourself) is the unabashed conviction of one's goodness, borderlining on textbook narcissism, that seems to be a prerequisite. Of course, I come to the table a self-doubter; if I had my wife's righteousness, I would be a dangerous individual, and possibly a Jew for Jesus. But it's more complicated than that: in an unguarded moment, she once revealed herself to be Cassandra (a not uncommon female symptom); you know, the (prettiest—that's part of the attraction) daughter of Priam who warned him that he had better look a Trojan horse in the mouth, and quick, but he wouldn't listen, supposedly because she had been cursed, but truly because of all the warnings she had issued previously ("the sea will boil on Tuesday, and your navy shall be cooked"). Being a local version of the unheeded prophetess has got to be something of a burden, but if she had insider information that things were going to go this way, wouldn't she have done something to prevent it? I would've, but I'm just a male; I didn't have the slightest idea what I was getting into; biologically I can't afford to think about it. I thought it was going to be okay. If you had told me I was going to marry a nay-saying soothsayer, I wouldn't have believed you (and you'd have to fight her for the Cassandra crown); if once the sooth she said appeared to hold something for me, I might believe it.

I have couples who come to my show, married sixty-five years, happy, cute; they look alike, seemingly living proof that the disparities of intermarriage (a man to a woman) can be overcome. I bet on the car ride home she reams him good:

"Why did you have to tell him that?"

"Because we did meet in a tavern. And I did see your sister first."

"None of his business. I need the world to know my business?

Mr. Comedian. You think you're funny. You're not funny. My sister doesn't think you're funny. She never did."

From there I imagine things quickly proceed to how I'm not funny either, possibly an anti-Semitic remark if they're not Semitic, followed by her daring him to find somebody else if he thinks anybody will still have him and culminating in an unintentionally blissful thirty-six hours of shunning, as if, after sixty-five years, it's going to teach him a lesson. He, of course, has long realized he is paying for marrying above himself, since that's all there is to marry, so be it, and maybe goes to see if they could use somebody at Mike's Super Subs in the mall a few days a week. Maybe they made it this far because, whatever she is, she isn't a screamer—that makes a difference. From the beginning, my wife screamed things to my face that I wouldn't have said behind my back. If half of what she's said about me is true, I'm missing some major organs, and a CAT scan would reveal nothing. Fortunately, I had an inflated ego to begin with, or I wouldn't have the men's medium I wear now. That I can face myself at all is only because it's easier than facing her. Still, if I am not worthy, how does she have the gall to cash the checks?

I don't know, I'm still a little rattled after being read this morning's riot act. I went into the Stop and Rob afterward and had to unload on Nino:

"I'm up at 6:30 making lunches. Ellie takes hers, pulls out most of the stuff. Nora has forgotten to do her homework again ('I hate myself! I hate myself'); I help her write out the list of 'logies' (pathology—'I don't know, I think it's dead people'), and we plug them into the crossword (which must wire vocabulary words into your brainstem, educationally theoretically speaking); then I have to drive her because she's late. Meanwhile, Cassandra, who prophesied that she would have to bake two sweet potato pies (despite being white and from the north) but did not believe herself, has yet to put them in the oven before scurrying off to work on her long day (out of *three*), saying, 'Take them out of the oven in an hour, or when the top starts to get flecks of brown; let it cool for an hour, and take it over to Nora's school.'

"'I can't . . . I don't have the time this morning. I need to be at work at eight. I told you about this week.'

"'This is not for me; this is for your daughter.' (Here comes the prophecy.) 'You will never care about anybody other than yourself.' Frankly, if I don't care about anybody other than myself; I'm sleeping 'til nine.

"I'm screaming back that hers is not the only valuable time; she non-sequiturs that she does a lot, or rather that she does not *not* do nothing, even though I never said she did *did,* and all but calls me a deadbeat dad . . ."

"Mine, too," says Nino. "They're all like that."

24

My Parents Smoke Pot

Ellie quickly picked everything off her slice of deluxe pizza, gnawed it up to the crust, and pushed back from the table to spring up out of her chair for the careen up to her room. "I can't have something to eat with you anymore," she said. "You explain too much."

What I just overexplained was that her mother and I had both smoked pot at some point in our otherwise uneventful (I speak for myself here) lives. I did have to explain to her that pot was marijuana, so that was good, that it was all in the past (not quite true, what with my corneas ripening), and that it is the worst thing ever for kids in their formative years. I didn't try to paint a picture of "the '70s" for her because I don't even believe it happened myself, but she's seen the clothes and the hair on *Three's Company,* so maybe she has an inkling.

This all came down, as we used to say, because we shared a Coke. "It's really something—there used to be cocaine in Coke, " Ellie said, to which I said yes, it really was. I was never a cokehead, although, like the president, I may have come into contact with it once or

99

twice before finding Jesus. "No wonder they sold so much of it, " she added, showing some marketing acumen that bodes well.

"It was legal at the time," I told her, adding that so was marijuana, or *cannabis sativa,* so naturally she wondered why it had been made illegal. I gave her the brief Harry Anslinger *Reefer Madness* overview and some sense that it was part of an earlier campaign to stamp out evil, or at least evils. At such times, I like to be as honest as I am comfortable with being as the aging (in)version of the same guy who, after his first semester away at college, made his mother sit and listen to a summary of his sex and drug life at the University of Wisconsin–Madison, fall semester, 1967. Every time Mom tried to pop up to get away from more than she ever wanted to know, I gently pushed her back down onto the kitchen chair, saying it was important to me that she know this.

Now my daughter was sitting at the table.

"You know, I've smoked pot." I added, "In my day."

"What's pot?"

"Marijuana. Weed." Ellie has seen those public service ads where the kid's mother takes away his cell phone because he smoked some weed, even though he says it wasn't that good.

"Everybody did in those days. Instead of beer."

"Dude." she said. "Was it legal?"

"No. Not exactly. For a while it was just a 5-dollar fine in Madison. Your mother has even smoked pot."

"Mother!" she screamed, steaming into the living room, where her mother was trying to make Nora watch *The Miracle Worker.* "Did you smoke marijuana?"

"Oh, I took a couple of puffs. Years ago."

"Mom! You're illegal."

"I don't do it now," she said. "Why did you tell Ellie I smoke pot?" she said, obviously needing to chill out.

"Because I said I had, and she wanted to know about you," I lied, illustrating one of the best indicators of long-term use.

"People!" Ellie said, before stomping up the stairs like she does (it's the what-we-would-have-called platforms). "I could turn you in! Hah!"

I think she was kidding, but these are the moments that always remind me of that little girl chewing on her daddy's leg in *Night of the Living Dead*. She always was a daddy's girl. Let them get the moral high ground, this is what happens. If nothing else, it does give Ellie another card to play alongside her old standby, "Touch me and I'll dial 911 so fast it'll make your head spin."

III

A Personality

25

Fame (I'm Gonna Live Forever)

I had a tête-à-tête with the man who told Sally Jessy to get red frames and had lunch with the man who conceived *Saved by the Bell*. Letterman whispered into my ear during a commercial break ("I was in Madison, once," he said, "in January." "Good timing," I said), and when I told Leno I knew a guy on his writing staff, he quipped, "Lucky for you." I had to wait for a dominatrix to finish with him before I could meet Donahue. When I shook Johnny Carson's hand while he was in undershirt and makeup bib and told him that I had stolen the format for my radio show from *Do You Trust Your Wife?* he said, "We all steal out here." On more than one occasion, Bryant Gumbel has laughed at something I've said. A guy from HBO Productions and Ellen DeGeneres's brother waited for me in the Century City Hilton lobby for hours and left because the guy at the desk didn't know I was staying there. NFL Films was interested.

Paramount called. I was handled, briefly, by the same speaking agency as General Schwartzkopf.

During the best fish meal (sea bass) I ever had, at Le Bernardin, in New York, I told the head of NBC that the one kind of TV show I wouldn't do was one where SWAT teams broke down doors to wrestle down and shackle black men in the name of entertainment, and he replied that his problem was he couldn't find enough of those shows, left to take a teleconference, and flipped the bill to the Chicago affiliate. I just missed meeting de Niro. Did I mention I did some TV shows from Oprah's studio (although she wasn't around)? I had my own entertainment lawyer at $250 an hour; fortunately, my career ran just ten hours. I stuffed bacon, eggs, and pancakes (a two-by-four, we call it here) into my face while taking a breakfast with several producers in Burbank who just sat with tea and didn't even touch their buns. At another meeting, a producer put his hands together into a frame and hunkered down to view me, and I actually worked with a director who wore a viewfinder with a largely unbuttoned jungle-print shirt. I myself still wear articles of wardrobe from several unsuccessful television projects. I have had dressers, at least one of whom was gay and caused me to look quite a little more flamboyant than usual, been spackled by the same makeup artist as Pamela Anderson, and discussed notes with network executives. I've been packaged.

During a fall TV season rollout in Burbank, I told a ballroom full of television reporters that, since I'd taught high school, a roomful of critics was nothing new to me. I met the man who invented the Coney Dog and the Wall from Wall Drugs. If immediate family counts, Sophie Tucker once sat on my father's lap during an Israel Bond fund drive. I worked a cable awards ceremony with Alan Thicke, who said he'd let Time-Warner know about me. He didn't, or he did and they didn't care. I signed my name on the table at Kroch's and Brentano's Bookstore in Chicago right next to Mickey

Mantle's. Steve Allen wrote a song about me that went, "I kvelled and I kvelled / About Tuesday Weld / But not about Feld-man." Disney had me under contract. The Tribune Company had me under contract ("One-sided boiler plate," my Chicago lawyer, Harvey Sussman, told me. "Sign it"). I was pursued by somebody who claimed to be from William Morris. Christian Broadcasting called. Lifetime for Women thought about making an exception for me. Twice producers I worked with on failed pilots went on to broadcast television success. I signed a two-book deal with a major publisher. Judith Regan called me from her hotel room.

I was this close to Dick Clark and Andy Williams, and, it's true, time marches on for us all: when I shook Little Richard's hand I couldn't help but notice his dark purple makeup ended right under his chin. Johnny Mathis was at Spago the same time I was. I got the dirt on Jamie Lee Curtis and Richard Gere from a genuine Hollywood type, although I still don't see how it's physically possible in either case. When I was introduced to David Lynch at a party, I couldn't squeeze out a word before he left to get his ears candled. Harry Carey once introduced me to the crowd from the booth at Wrigley Field, and I piloted the Goodyear blimp over Akron. My suite at the Cleveland Clinic hotel was the same one used by the late King Faisal of Saudi Arabia, I followed Bill into the Governor's Suite at the Excelsior in Little Rock, and I was Honorary Duckmaster at the Peabody in Memphis right after Hillary. When I was considered upcoming, *People* magazine ran a spread for which the photographer suggested my wife and I get in a bubble bath like the astronaut Deke Slayton and his did. We didn't. I was considered for *Later*. Chris Darden and I were on the same panel. I rode in a limo that still smelled of Michelle Pfeiffer. I was the Parade Marshal for the Wisconsin Badgers 2000 Homecoming Game against Purdue. They lost. I'm sure there's more that I can't even remember.

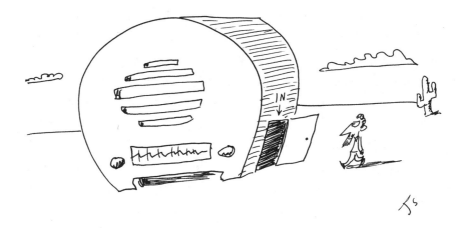

26

How to Get into Radio

As a grizzled if not wizened radio veteran, I have been approached by more than one youngster with a not yet jaundiced eye on my enviable job, wondering how they, too, can host a comedy-quiz show on public radio. Remembering my encounter with the great Garrison Keillor many years back (when, after I regaled him after a show with tales of my formative broadcasts from a Madison greasy spoon, he asked me where the men's room was), I try to forget my bladder and come up with some feasible way he or she might get into the business, but the fact is, like so much else in an underplanned life with no clear objectives, I just kind of stumbled over it while looking in another direction. Had I taken courses in television and radio, they doubtless would've discouraged me, as courses in advertising, political science, and even philosophy (logic—not my cup of tea) had from further study and the slim hope of gainful employment in fields that don't really exist. Hey, it's college. Being an English speaker, of a sort, I was an English major by default, and a high school English teacher by what choice there was—I mean, what else are you going to do with an English degree? True, I had won a couple of contests as a kid in Milwaukee, getting to yammer and play "Louie, Louie" on our two rock stations; the station manager of one told me to forget about it and go to college, good advice that I took. In the back of my head, I must have thought I could do radio, which really requires only that you not clam up in front of a mike and renounce any higher expectations of yourself, but the War at Home and the subsequent peace dividend, which you had to invest in finding something to do with your life, soon drove any such thoughts from my mind.

Radio is not necessarily a higher pursuit. Not a lot of idealists are driven to it, although those that are, Christian broadcasters aside, naturally end up in public radio, where stations still speak of their "mission," as if it were from God and not the University Extension. Back in the 1970s, when the need to express yourself became a pandemic, it seemed like an easy way to go. The FM band, before everything was programmed from Texas, was, like the Internet until recently, pretty much of a free-for-all of music, personalities, and even ideas. There were possibilities if a guy knew how to take advantage of them; fortunately, I didn't, or I might be doing afternoons in Corpus Christi right now. Sometimes you just have to approach things with the best of un-intentions: my little break came when, while teaching English at an alternative high school and suffering my annual Christmas depression (I was between wives and getting diminishing returns from teaching, which, no one told me, involves attempting to change the habits of roomfuls of teenagers), I volunteered at a local listener-sponsored (you pay, we play) station, WORT, which, as the call letters suggest, had been started by a couple of émigré New Yorkers several years before. WORT was (and still is) one of those quasi cooperatives, like the food coops or the cab company (Union Cab) I would eventually be a local celebrity driver for, that are actually run by a few people with varying degrees of clandestine management skill but that, in the case of the station, empowered many with bad voices who would otherwise not have gotten the chance in a million years to play Peruvian pan flute music or call Dizzy, Charlie, and Earl by their first names on the airwaves. Volunteering, which was uncharacteristic, I was offered the chance to deliver the Back Porch Pilot, station listings that aspired to street journalism, since I still had my three-quarter-ton pickup from the former day-camp lifetime. This was too cooperative for me, and I was forced to demur.

I came back at some point with some vox pops I had made on campus with the deck I had bought to record my friend John's gigs, and the program director (surprisingly, there was one), Jeff Lange, was impressed enough to let me fill in the odd Friday night call-in for the bedridden or undatable, and he eventually to ask me to do a morning show, previously accomplished by five separate individuals working in five distinct genres, every morning, straight across, Monday through Friday. (This strip programming, stinking of commercialism, of course, pissed off everybody off from the wimmin's music people to those who held in earnest public servitude, and the bad feelings lingered. Last I heard, Jeff was a Realtor.) I took it on with the stipulation that the show be a live remote, knowing that without an audience I wouldn't bother to perform; the result, the Breakfast Special from Dolly's Fine Foods, under the sign of the dancing hamburger (I still have the salvaged sign; at ground level, the legs turned out to be tomato slices), is personal history. Starting at six, I would extemporize before my id had awakened, interview hapless folks in the diner between bouts of John Prine and Fathead Newman played from the station, and, at nine, pack up to see if anybody had turned up for "Carlos Castaneda and the Literature of the Seeker" at Shabazz Alternative High School. Eventually, when it became clear that talking was easier than talking and motivating, I quit teaching and devoted myself to the high calling of waking people up. When, after a couple of years, I couldn't abide the managers (I would learn, years later, that in radio management, only the diameter of the asshole changes [with market share] but at the time I was naïve), I finished up a fund drive one morning, played Elvis Costello's "Clown Time Is Over," and quit on-air on air (something I would recommend against, or maybe just once for the rush) for the much more challenging opportunity of using a microphone while delivering passengers from the far west side (Madison has a street named Grand Teton; news to me) to the airport. It was while driving cab that I got the call from Jack Mitchell, the head of Wisconsin Public Radio, asking me to come by and talk about maybe doing something over there, as well as an invitation to come down to the Hancock Building in Chicago to fail to impress the ABC Radio blue suits who had just fired Steve Dahl for the second time. Eventually I would get a chance to fail all on my own in Chicago radio (it's a long, long way from WORT to WGN), before returning to Madison with the idea for a comedy-quiz show with a live audience, a little combo for musical interludes, and a quiz that would allow me to put people on the air without having to talk about anything of importance, in time making me, according to *The Wall Street Journal,* at least when they anointed me, "the king of small talk radio."

And that, kids, is how you do it. Take what you think you can use, and press on—or, better yet, go to college and forget about it.

27

Whad'ya Know?

I had a terrible thing happen to me the other year—I turned fifty. I raged against the lengthening of the shadows by maintaining a low-grade, long-term depression and forbade a fiftieth birthday party, which would mean the inevitable gag gifts. I thought I was home free when, on the weekend of my birthday, of all people my radio audience brought me every one of those gag gifts. Amazingly, it worked. I felt much better, particularly in the Depends. This is the beauty of Midwestern humor—it brings you back to earth. This is also the beauty of having an audience; everyone should have one. Still, it is a responsibility, even if I'm not the "empty vessel" ("Fill me!") I claim. Art Linkletter was right: people are funny. It's just spotty. And kids are the darndest things; sometimes saying nothing at all, perhaps because they're six months old and holding back, preferring to drool over a microphone while trying to stuff it into their faces. In the warm-up, I tell them, "This is an audience participation show—if it's a bad show, whose fault is it? Inevitably, of course, they say, "Yours!" (it's a rare audience that accepts responsibility), but, frankly, without them I'm pretty much twisting up there. Our people come primarily from Wisconsin (including the Upper Peninsula, which, by rights, should be ours, anyway), Minnesota, Illinois, and Iowa, with more adventurous souls showing up from Missouri, Michigan, Ohio, and Azerbaijan. It was the guy from Azerbaijan, Ozzer, a student in international finance, who wondered "what the deal was with Mary in all the bathtubs around here?" referring to the common Wisconsin practice (particularly in Kenosha, where it is an art) of using the old bathtub from a conversion to bury on end in the backyard as a religious grotto. It was then that I began to think that maybe we were special. Was there a Midwestern sensibility, a worldview, a characteristically good-natured, deadpanned irony? I'm no sociologist, but see if you can draw any conclusions from some of the things people have said on the show:

Duncan, from Wauwatosa, was still mourning the loss of his beloved pickup truck:

"What possessed you to sell it?"

"It didn't run anymore."

"You could have parked it on the lawn."

"She wouldn't let me. The washer and the dryer are in the way."

Ours is a surprisingly diverse crowd. Take Brian from West Bend, "not an environmentalist but a Republican" and a "logistics specialist" (truck driver) who "hauls a lot of cheese" and was in Madison for the Haitian festival. Samuel, originally from Kenya, shows how completely he has become acculturated as the city chemist at the sewage plant in Oshkosh: "I try to be friends with everybody in Oshkosh so they'll keep flushing." While putting up high-moisture corn in his silo, John, a dairy farmer from western Wisconsin, paused to call in the finishing touch for a young woman's paper on Dante's *Inferno,* which we were helping her write on air: "Beatrice showed him heaven and Virgil showed him hell." Kelly got 100 percent on her paper.

We own hydrogeologists, ministers, and rural mail carriers. When a woman from New Glarus pulled a garlic sausage from her purse and I remarked, "This cries out for a beer!" a mail carrier delivered one before the end of the show. While I can't explain the hydrogeologists, the ministers are obviously looking for material for Sunday, and the rural mail carriers can listen on their routes, like Dave from Strum (near Osseo), who took a day off to come down and play the quiz:

"Where would you be about now, Dave?"

"Going down the hill by Craig Potter's place."

"Is he keeping it up pretty good?"

"He lives quite a ways off the road, so it really doesn't matter."

"That's a lot for him to keep up, the Potter place—I heard he's thinking of selling it off."

"With a driveway like that, I'd consider it, too."

"The county won't plow it."

"No—only if he'd leave a few more presents at Christmas."

"That how it works with the mail, too?"

"No, you'd get it anyway. Eventually."

You learn about jobs in my job—I mean what people really do. Shawn, a systems analyst for the Department of Natural Resources, admitted that that meant he "watched fish grow." A biological mass spectrometrist by trade, Chris ionizes brain molecules for analysis, but, when pinned down, he reveals that "it's just dosing people with a lot of drugs and seeing what happens." The people skills learned on the job by Ron, a paramedic with the fire department, start with not saying, "You idiot, what did you call us for?" Donna writes computer software programs for insurance agents: "Here is your desk. On your right you'll see a drawer. You could put files in that." Charles, an unusually candid pest control expert, reveals that those who fail the pest control exam "get to be pest control experts" and that "we tell our customers who are concerned about the humaneness of our job that we take the mice out alive and release them in the forest preserve. Technically we release them to another customer." In the aftermath of the Monica Lewinsky laundry problems, Susan, a dry cleaner from Medford, Wisconsin, admitted, "We put the 'We Did the Best We Could' cards on every other garment," while her husband, a long-distance trucker, confirmed what many had long suspected: "I park at truck stops, but I eat at restaurants."

Then there are the slices of life. Sarah, who was getting married the next day, was in the audience while her fiancé was priming for the football game in the bars along State Street. Why? "My dad really wanted the wedding to be on a football weekend," she explained. Her dad claimed he was promoting "the synergy between community life and personal life." A heating and cooling engineer from Waukesha, Larry grows flowers for his wife ("It works, guys!") and "tomatoes for myself. There's the difference between us in a nutshell." Molly, a young woman just thirty days into living with her boyfriend, wonders "Why do all bachelors have Buddhas?" when they are, in fact, Lutheran. Julie and Debbie, on a self-described Thelma and Louise weekend, "picked up two guys on campus last night—but it was dark and they couldn't tell how old we were." Maternal pride was epitomized by Doris, who said of her son, Ed, who was sitting in the audience, that "he finished school, stayed out of jail, and has a steady job. What more could I ask?" Dan, from Iowa, says he doesn't play Powerball because his church, the United Methodist, "says I can't tell anybody if I win." Randy, a farmer near Janesville, built a cornfield maze ("a maize maze") in the shape of the state of Wisconsin with a tower in it from which to look for lost souls and to "help people in distress, but I can't handle all their problems." Asked the secret of being married to Janice for fifty years, Cliff said simply, "We pound our wrinkles out from the inside, one at a time." And Katherine, a ten-year-old who showed up in a gingham dress and bonnet from "old-fashioned days" at her school, explained that

that's where "you sit around and use slates and the teachers never compliment you."

Richard, who complained one day that with his wife it was "Michael Feldman this, Michael Feldman that," was, I hope, listening when Michael Feldman, age ten, showed up and said the name was not confusing because "lots of people don't even know who you are." There you go.

28

Michael Feldman
Discovered America In ...

Nineteen eighty-eight, when, searching for the headwaters of Ames, Iowa, he discovered that Jim Packard, announcer and interim producer, had actually booked our rooms in Des Moines, a hair-raising forty-five minutes away on I-35. We did a show at the Iowa State University (home of the Swine Research Center, which may or may not have housed the behemoth hog Jane Smiley describes in Moo U), even though the high art concept of *Whad'ya Know?,* the national show heard in three places outside Wisconsin (this being one), was still so new that even the people from the station failed to show up. Years later, when we did a show in Des Moines (Jim had relinquished his position; that time, we meant to be in Des Moines and even had on Jane Smiley to attempt to nail down the Hog of the Apocalypse rumor), the station showed up to apologize and collect ticket money. Like Vietnam, we claimed that Iowa had invited us, but we couldn't prove it; today we have normalized relations (although there still is

North Iowa). We were first there during the caucuses, which is what you call it when white people select candidates, when the prevailing joke was you could tell where the candidates had been stumping because the corn was taller. Piglets get so used to being held during the primary that they're ruined for life and are good only for picture opportunities (which, for an old hog, get few and far between). I really like Iowans; they're like Wisconsinites but without an ax to grind. The only thing that bothers me about them is they will never tell you where they're from; it's always from Iowa, which covers a host of sins, and will never admit to Toolesboro or Wapello. They won't be pinned down, those Hawkeyes, and you can't blame an outsider for thinking they're hiding something.

After Ames, we raided Northfield, Minnesota, and, unlike the James Gang, came back with all our ears. I saw what is purported to be Jesse James's ear, and, like many relics, you can't really tell what it actually is—it could be another body part altogether that the city fathers were reluctant to name but that would've resulted in a lot more foot traffic. I had my first lutefisk in Northfield, and I can truly say I haven't had any since, and certainly no hankering. Lefse either. Matzoh at least God made us eat. Northfield is a Lutheran prairie outpost (unlike, say, Carleton; we did our show in the chapel right where they lay out the body, but we were mostly able to work around that). Naturally I relished the thought of a Jew on the pulpit in a Lutheran church as sweet revenge for all the abuse heaped on me by my Missouri Synod–incited childhood friends; later I worked the chapel at Carthage College, in Kenosha, and a Unitarian meeting house in Grand Rapids, which, with the stained glass windows and all, looked like a church to me. (If they had locked the doors and burned the place, they would have gotten rid of every liberal in town.) The Lutherans are very nice to me now, on the road and at home, and it's a rare audience that doesn't hold one or two pastors looking for material and, as parishioners have confirmed, planning to use it without accreditation. The radio folks in Northfield are the David to Minnesota Public Radio's Goliath; they are of hardy stock and took us in as one of their own early on. It's a pretty town right out of Main Street, USA, and has a boarding house, the Archer House, on whose porch W. C. Fields might have slept (at least until the bowling ball came bounding down the stairs).

They say you can't go back, and Milwaukee proves it, even though by the time we did our first *Whad'ya Know?* show in my hometown, Mom had been motherknapped by my brother Arthur, flown to California, and forced to do arts and crafts in a Santa Clara residential center. Aunt Rose was still doing pretty well, though — she was at the show, although shyer on mike than her little sister Gerry had been at her height, when you had to pull her offstage to make her stop with the homilies. Mayor Norquist came on to sing "Roll Out the Barrel," before we found out what barrel he was rolling, as was the man who was synonymous with Milwaukee nightlife for years, Louis Bashell, the polka king. It was here I delivered my "Ich bin ein Milwaukeean" speech ("they think they've seen edged lawns, let them come to Milwaukee . . ."), which coincided with the tearing down of the Berlin Wall and the suspension of demolition for the northwest freeway, unfortunately, long after the threat of condemnation forced Mom to sell out for peanuts. Fortunately, she likes peanuts. The Michael Feldman Story — Milwaukee to Madison in only three decades. People say I've come a long way, but seventy-two miles in thirty years is 2.4 miles per year or .0003 miles per hour. Talk about life in the fast lane. And, in a few years, Waukesha will grow to meet Madison's east side, and I'll be back in Milwaukee, where I started from. Brookfield, a sleepy little village where I used to take my first carsick stop on County 18 on the way to see Howie at the UW, now looks like San Jose. There's twelve lanes of traffic, but, of course, everyone still drives like a Milwaukeean: "with ear flaps," as my dad used to say. Milwaukeeans think that if God wanted them to merge with traffic, He would've created a hole large enough for them to do it. High-occupancy vehicle lanes have never caught on because every guy coming back from up north with a deer on the fender thinks he qualifies.

The city of Milwaukee is still losing population, but, being Milwaukeeans, people don't go that far. Mukwonago or Pewaukee, maybe, or Main Street in Menomonee Falls near Ernie Von Schladehorn, a modern-day Noah who has gathered one (despite the volume, they do not mate) of every kind of vehicle for sale. Most Milwaukeeans these days do not live in Milwaukee at all but in Brown Deer, Bayside, or Mequon, all formerly assumed to be uninhabitable. Mequon used to be where your parents threatened to send you if you were bad; now people live entire lives there. Poles still tend to pool up on the south side and African Americans on the north, but the 27th Street viaduct is no longer referred to as the biggest bridge in the world for connecting Poland to Africa. The Jews have pretty much left the west side, where we grew up so tantalizingly close to Wauwatosa and the Holy Angel's girls. That's what the Milwaukee Passover is all about—the exodus of the Jews to Fox Point. If you've sinned, you go to Bayside. Every ethnic group now has its own heaven within commuting distance of the Cream City.

Springfield, Missouri, is very nearly the crossroads of America, where north doesn't quite meet south and east stops well short of west, and all of it belongs to John Q. Hammons, who, going the Creator one better, put his name on it all. Nobody I asked seems to have heard the bang that started it all, but I bet it was big; we played at the Juanita Q. Hammons Performing Arts Center, no coincidence. There is an ungodly number of churches, Baptist and beyond, in Springfield, as well as Evangel College and the National Assemblies of God. Everybody else would do well to hunker down during the Rapture; the horizon over Springfield will be crowded. I think it's mostly out-of-towners who are proselytizing, but, you know, I met mostly public radio types in my several trips there, and they tend to be secular humanists, or fallen-away Protestants, if that's possible. Something akin to religion goes on in Missouri's Mecca, nearby Branson, where Shoji Tabuchi, besides being able to play the fiddle hanging from his feet from a Piper Cub (something he doesn't do during the show; even the new theater, while bigger, is not that big) has built a ladies room so plush that busloads of gentlewomen from Arkansas hold it all the way from Fort Smith to set a spell there, and this is long after plumbing became commonplace in Arkansas. Branson used to be a fishing hole; they still have striped bass, but now they have their own theater. If you think you're washed up, I have two words for you: Moe Bandy. Andy Williams sang "Moon River" so many times in Branson, it's now wider than 387,456 miles. I was looking at a site myself just outside Mutton Hollow.

Springfield is the kind of town where you can leave your keys in your car and have a 78 percent chance of finding them there when you get back. Otherwise, I would look for them in Kansas. People actually leave their doors unlocked so that they won't have to replace the window should somebody from Galena, Kansas, break in. The city motto was getting worked on when I was down there: "Everywhere should be like this," which, to my ear, sounds a little too much like what my mother used to say: "Everybody should be as good as me." Springfield has a teeny bit of an image problem since upstart Branson affixed its name to the airport, as well as just being lost among the horde of Springfields around the country. The first time we flew in, the pilot said, "This is flight 7032 bound for Springfield . . ." and everybody on board shouted "Missouri!" We ate at the Bass Pro Shop, where it's possible to pick your own large mouth from the aquarium and have a couple of guys in a bass boat haul him out for your dinner, although it can take a while if they're not biting. We've done shows in Springfield three or four times, because Arlen Diamond, the station manager at KSMS, is still trying to make some money on us after we forced him to charge only five bucks in '89 and at the same time managed, while fidgeting with it, to lose his diamond ring under the bleachers, to boot. He's a nice guy, though, and eventually it's going to pay off.

Paul Simon, the former senator from Illinois (who, sadly, died recently), was voted the prettiest boy baby in Eugene, Oregon, in 1932. Just off the top of my head, you ask? Well, yes, but only because I studied in Carbondale, Illinois, where Senator Simon directed the Public Policy Institute at Southern Illinois University. If it hadn't come up, say, right off the bat, when I interviewed him, I would have been surprised. What can you say—pretty babies grow up, and there's no guarantee. I have to say I am a star in Carbondale (and in Charleston, West Virginia, but that's about it), where people, many of whom appeared to still be of child-bearing age, stopped me on the street and quoted me to me. Starved for entertainment? Perhaps, but also very appreciative. Carbondale and all of greater Little Egypt remain very much on my mind, partly because there are so many unanswered questions: Why is Southern Illinois known as Egypt? Is it the delta thing with your Mississippi, your Ohio, and your Wabash confluence? Is it the pyramidal mounds left behind by an earlier civilization? Has evidence been unearthed, separate plate shards and seder platters, that there were once Jews? It may be the local predilection to sail into the hereafter in cardboard skiffs (for this is the home of the Cardboard Regatta). Nobody knows, but if the other Egypt had the Illinois Central instead of the Suez, they might pronounce it Kay-ro, too.

As is my wont on our road trips, I did look for evidence of the first Jewish civilization (this goes back to my mother's tendency to send me clippings supporting her thesis that "there are Jews everywhere"), which seems to have dawned in Carbondale in 1894, with the advent of Solomon and Winters—One-Price Cash Clothiers, established by J. J. Winters of nearby Du Quoin and J. Solomon of (where else) Chicago, who set up shop, appropriately enough, in the Odd Fellows building (the parallels to my father's disastrous credit-clothing foray in Racine with his Odd Fellow lodge partner, Izzy, are inescapable). A Mr. John Lethem, who chronicled the early days, noted that "here one will find a large and varied line of goods neatly and tastefully arranged so as to give one every opportunity of making a selection," adding, quite unnecessarily, "Mr. J. J. Winters is the resident member of the firm." You can take Solomon out of Chicago, but, it seems, you can't take Chicago out of Solomon.

Carbondale is the first city I've run across that lists a daytime and a nighttime population (49,000 and 27,000 respectively), reflecting not merely the hardiness of the 27,000 who stick it out but the comparative size of the Southern Illinois student body and the fact that it departs, at dusk, for parts unknown, Murphysboro, perhaps, or Beaucoup (pronounced "Bow-kup," like in Yiddish—a Solomon legacy?). SIU has the Small Business Incubator, where fledgling businesses are kept at a constant 105 degrees until they hatch; Senator Simon's Public Policy Institute, which, like the Senator, seems to be concerned about everything; and a medical school that attracted unwanted national attention a few years ago when its long-standing policy, since repealed, of cutting the legs off used cadavers so that they would ship in a smaller box (34 inches) broke in *The Daily Egyptian*. What no one talks about is that the cadavers were going to Chicago, possibly to vote in the primaries.

All around is the beautiful Shawnee National Forest, which has more than twenty varieties of wild orchids, more trees than all of Europe, and 85 percent of all types of vertebrates. If it's vertebrates, you're after, look no further. Over the years, SIU has garnered a reputation as a party school, although the College Guide assures readers that "academics have priority during the week, but students report that Wednesday, Thursday, Friday, and Saturday nights are reserved for partying."

Portland, Oregon, is one of those places that's impossible not to like, even though they don't want you to, because you might stay. First thing they ask you at Portland immigration is "How long are you staying?" "Are you carrying any concealed fruits, nuts, or Californians?" "Do you plan on leaving the urban growth boundary for any reason?" Actually, I believe in a no-growth area. In fact, I wish I had one other than the one on my scalp. Where else but in Portland, except maybe Eugene, would you see the headline "Study Hints Tide of Newcomers Has Begun to Ebb"? Fewer refugees, apparently, are slipping in. There's no room at the inn. Obviously, that's what this assisted-suicide thing is all about. The fact is, if you are a former Californian, you are three times as likely to be offered assisted suicide. That's the untold story here. I don't understand this whole Proposition 51; your doctor already has the right to kill you. It's called health care. And, if your family doctor won't kill you, you have the right to go to an HMO or sit in a waiting room until you expire. I believe in death with dignity, which is why I've asked not to be laid out in a clown suit. Until then, a little life with dignity would be a good thing, I think. But I don't want to meddle in local prerogatives.

I hesitate to say they have a beautiful town, that it combines green space and hills with unmatched river vistas and the best in the ergo-urban living experience. That it conveys a social consciousness and values found in few other places—because I know they don't want the word to get out. So let me just mention property taxes and the weather. Actually, 277 cloudy days would not be a lot if the year were 600 days long, like on some planets. Of course, those planets don't have property taxes. But, I don't care what anybody says, rain is not liquid sunshine. Portlanders just have to get past that. Liquid sunshine would be more like magma—which they do have, barely contained, so they may be right after all. I, for one, never assume that a volcano is extinct as long as it's within city limits. Not everybody's lucky enough to have Mount St. Helens right down the block.

And she was supposed to be extinct, wasn't she? The fact is Portland could be the next Pompeii, with fleeing Portlanders preserved in the lava in Gore-Tex ponchos, hiking shorts, and Birkenstocks: like the Pompeians, unable to escape due to footwear. Even if they're wearing Nikes, the next swoosh they hear may be their own, and that little berm out in Beaverton isn't going to save them. Portland is the only place I've been to that operates on a rain year. I've heard of calendar years and fiscal years, but here the rain year ends on September 30, and I believe that for every drop of rain that falls, a microbrewery grows. How many India Pale Ales do you need? I like a microbrew, but you've got to drink a lot of them. Beer and coffee and rain, all chemically similar, all in harmonious balance. Sitting under the canopy in Pioneer Square drinking double lattes and then walking around underdressed for the drizzle, saying, "At least it's not raining" gives you a taste of the Portland experience; then just move along, perhaps to Seattle.

We played in Peoria, except for the unfortunate choice of a newspaper columnist who, apparently, didn't much like his current assignment and has probably been laid off at Caterpillar by now. But, for me, Peoria will always be Big Al's. It was inevitable, being right next to the hotel and all. When you mention Peoria, particularly to a salesman, he inevitably says, "Been to Big Al's?" and now I know why. Al's is a family-oriented strip club that has been grandfathered into the Peorian moral sensibility, which, at the time we were there, had gotten its back up entirely against a Hooter's going in—a woman dangling from a pole by her foot is one thing, but one in a T-shirt, shorts, and panty hose is quite another (and I have no idea what goes on at Oogies). I was not there to judge, or to get lap danced, because I really don't need to pay to be that uncomfortable in front of a woman. All seemed like good clean fun to me, though, because that's just the Big Al's way. At this point, I would like to mention the Peoria Ballet, Player's Theater, Symphony, Civic Chorale, and Opera, plus the Corn Stock Theater in Bradley Park, all tremendous cultural assets that just didn't happen to be next to our hotel, or I would've gladly stumbled into *Die Fledermaus* and stayed for hours buying watered-down drinks for the cast. If Aïda offered me a private dance, I just might go for it.

Although we'd be hard pressed to come up with a definition, Peoria seems to suffer just a bit from not being Normal, I guess because Bloomington/Normal got the air service; still there is direct air service to Bloomington/Normal and it's possible to get a bus to any major hub in the Midwest if that option doesn't sit well with you. A road to Chicago would be nice, one that doesn't hook up with 55, which is Bloomington's. Just a little diagonal between the Robert Michel and the Mike Royko bridges. Other than that, the only major news was Galesburg's intention to follow the Duchy of Grand Fenwick model—declare war on the United States and lose in order to get the foreign aid—I wouldn't be surprised, what with all the machine parts, if the guys at Caterpillar couldn't come up with a Q bomb.

New York City. I went there as a kid with my roommate Bob, and we tried to bring hookers back to our hotel room, getting as far as the doorman, who discerned that these girls were not paying guests. Or maybe it was us. Eventually, we figured it out, and I was over my nonspecific in a couple of weeks. Really cleaned up Times Square—would've never found a Virgin Superstore there in the old days. Your joke here. Anyway, I had a lot riding emotionally on returning to the Big Apple as Michael Feldman, which, along with a token at the time, would get you a ride out to Brooklyn on the subway, if you weren't taking the orthodox bus already. I remember the first time I made eye contact with a New Yorker, only to find out it was a blind guy at the newsstand. I'm used to women not looking at me, but when everybody does it you begin to take it personally. Walking down a Manhattan street is a real tribute to peripheral vision. Most people here didn't look up when Godzilla came through.

Going to New York, I always had the feeling that everybody was Jewish—Jets, Sharks, everybody—including Officer Krupke, but saying "dafen gansa college" to several Palestinians soon gets you over that. They might have been from the Emirates. It's like riding with a cabbie with his Islamic Jihad photo next to his ID—it's a melting pot. Once you realize it's the family back in Yemen they're talking to via those wire headphones, you relax 100 percent, except for the driving style, which comes from trying to shake off those clinging to the outside of the jitney.

It's not that I don't think I can't make it in New York; it's just that, even if I didn't, I could still make a pretty good living elsewhere. It wouldn't be burning in the back of my head, exactly. After all, I've wowed them wowed them, repeatedly, in Cleveland, and in Philadelphia I was no slouch. And at Town Hall, to think of the greats who played there, and Garrison, too, it was almost too much. Once I really wanted to make it in New York when I mistakenly believed the Round Table was still going on at the Algonquin, but it's pretty much just Bobby Short at the nearby Carlyle. Cats they have at the Algonquin, not the musical but actual cats, in the lobby. I stayed in the Dorothy Parker room and waited all night, but she never showed. But doing the show was a piece of cake, because every New Yorker, certainly those who came, is doing their own show—all you have to do is mike them, and I'm a seasoned professional; I can do that. They're all bursting with points of view, not all ill founded. They go through a lot and aren't afraid to tell you about it, something a Midwesterner can only mutely stand by and be befuddled about. My brother Arthur fell in a grease pit once and didn't say anything about it to the service station guy. Why? He's from the Midwest.

People always ask me if there's a city we've been in (and we've been in more than a hundred now) I like best, or a part of the country where people are most receptive, and I'd have to say in the South and the South, respectively. The South came as a surprise to me, since I'd never been below mid-Illinois, where they start automatically serving you grits with your eggs, but it's got a lot going for it as a region—the weather, of course, except during ice storms or hurricanes, and the people, outgoing, friendly, and helpful, when you can find 'em; unfortunately, most of the folks you run into when you do a public radio show are from Michigan, no matter where you go. When we finally played in Michigan, I was startled to see anyone was left. This is nothing against Wolverines; it's just that, if you're in Alabama, Mississippi, or South Carolina, you'd like to meet real Scarletts and Rhetts. Southern women are the best—they doll up, they look at you, and when they talk to you in their delicious argot they put their hand upon your arm, even with their husbands standing there. I thought I was inexplicably hot in Southern eyes until I realized that they do it to everyone, but, all in all, I didn't care. In the Midwest, a woman won't touch you even if she's married to you, and your beneficiary, so you've got to like that. The guys seem to expect it and don't mind, although it's hard to imagine not being threatened by the likes of me. The height of southern gentility is Charleston, South Carolina, where we were entertained in true Dixie fashion SOB (South of Broad) even though we were from "off." Charleston is arguably one of the most beautiful cities in America, although Charlestonians are too polite to argue it, with its Greco, Roman, Palladian, and Adams-like (they don't call it "Federal" down there) mansions nestled alongside a harbor so picturesque it's difficult to imagine cannonballs (one of which they left embedded in the church) from Fort Sumter flying over it during the Civil War— make that the War of Northern Aggression. They've got these "single houses" down there that are actually perpendicular to the street; the occupants practice what maybe the only thing with these words in it: "North side courtesy"—which means you avoid looking out a north-facing window, not because if you keep going you hit a Yankee but to avoid coveting your neighbor's piazza. You might see where they're burying their valuables, should the Union troops take a turn this way. One could imagine a worse lifestyle than taking a little place in Charles Towne—I've got my eye on the one the Calhouns used to have, assuming we're past that restrictive deed thing. I think they'd let me go on that one, but maybe not on the fact that I went to William T. Sherman grade school (even though Sherman decided to burn Columbia instead of Charleston, he's not regarded as a savior). The Citadel is here, training ground for many in the insurance industry; show the ring and you get 30 percent off term insurance. Even the Jews are genteel here. Religious tolerance marks Charleston's history, the oldest temple in the Americas being Beth Elohim, established in 1749.

Savannah had reform Jews before the rest of the country even had Jews. The police chief, an African American gentlemen, was Reuben Greenberg (I can hear my mother now: "Convert?" No, Mom, he was born black.). Savannah has been called the Holy City, which, admittedly, may be because of either the number of churches or the constant shelling. Or, consider Savannah, arguably the most beautiful city in America (see above), and even more Southern than Charleston. Sherman spared Charleston, but he ended up staying in Savannah. You have to like a place where the aloha is "What will you have to drink?" In Savannah, it was noon in the Garden of Good and Evil, and I was the Bird Boy at Clary's. I even met Lady Chablis, although she planted one on Jim, who didn't know how to feel about it. I see how she could shake up a cotillion. One thing I didn't get to do was crash the Married Women's Club, where the ladies still meet at 4:15 for drinks and cards. The men have the Oglethorpe Club, although the odds of my getting in there are about as great as my chances of crashing the MWC. Preston Russell, a historian who was on the show, said of Savannah, "The Jews own it, the Irish run it, and the crackers enjoy it"—although that pretty much insults everybody. Could work with it, although I could never stay long enough to be one of the old families; in fact, they might throw "The Book" (the social register, not the other testament) at me. I stink of new money. Johnny Mercer, who wrote every song you ever loved, as well as "Moon River," is from here, and, like him, you can finish your box of chocolates in Chippewa Square, sit on Conrad Aiken's bench in Bonaventure Cemetery, and take your martini straight up. We partied in a mansion on one of the squares, where our very cordial hosts—who dressed for cocktails while we showed up in shmatas—plied us with food and drink of a quality you just don't get tailgating—you can't blame me for hanging onto the door jamb when it was time to leave. And the thing about Savannah is that not only do they welcome you with open arms, but if they wrong you in some way, they'll "kiss your behind at Bull and Braughton and give you an hour to draw a crowd." You can't beat a deal like that.

29

Fan Base

I've met my biggest fans a number of times and found, surprisingly, that they never turn out to be all that big. Still, I guess I could stop saying that to them, just as I've resisted confiding that they might not be so enthusiastic if they really knew me—because, who knows, they might. I'm not a bad person—if I weren't privy to all my private thoughts and (in)actions, I might be my biggest fan, too. You can't afford to alienate your audience; my wife was a fan at one time (although, come to think of it, she never did say "biggest"); there's no surer way to lose one than to marry one (that's when the shit hits the fan) or to ignore someone who really wants to put a face to the voice. The one time, years ago, when I met Garrison Keillor after a show and told him all about my fledgling radio career broadcasting from a greasy spoon and he asked me where the men's room was sealed that for me. As a result, today, even if I have to go, I say, "That's really something!"

It's great to have fans, especially when you're this needy. You must be okay, after all, if you have fans, although Hitler certainly had his and Rush Limbaugh has a lot more than I ever will, barring some change in the American or Limbaugh's psyche. Having fans is humbling. Sometimes you have to pinch yourself, hard, if you like that sort of thing. When you first have fans, it can be a little weird because of all the attention you're suddenly getting, and how imperceptibly better it makes you feel about yourself. Everybody deserves fans. Why should the woman who single-handedly drives the green recycling truck *and* flings the bags up on top not have fans? She does, in me (you know the one I mean, the blonde who plays country music), but she'd have many more if she were syndicated. Most jobs don't elicit or require a fan base, of course, which is why most middle managers continue to work rather than being hung by their heels or pulled from the schedule due to flagging ratings. In my business, you don't have fans, you don't have work. People had better like me. A lot. The loyal ones will even stick with you your whole working life until you outgrow your demographic and become statistically unimportant together. That means a lot.

When you first have fans, it's easy to confuse them (and they you) with real people and even see them as being the ideal relationship—people who love you and go away. Maybe Howard Stern sees the women he fondles on-air off, and maybe not. I'd like to think not. It's best to keep the medium between you, where it belongs, and not actually try to enter through the shower radio. In public broadcasting, it's a moot point, anyway, unless you're attracted to middle-aged men who still live with their mothers and/or mothers who still have their middle-aged sons living with them. Norman Bates fit the public radio profile and would have found much on *All Things Considered* to consider. The rest, at least judging from those who can ambulate to our show, seem to be electrical engineers, hydrogeologists, graduate students in any number of disciplines, the stray dairy farmer, state office and university workers, rural mail carriers, lawyers (some of whom claim to be working in the public interest), ten-year-olds, insurance adjustors, and people who have something to do with a computer, either on the trash-in or trash-out side. If I've left anybody out, I apologize. Oh, and ministers, almost always in street wear, who (parishioners report) use my copyrighted material in sermons without attribution, unlike, say, the Lord God, Who always gets credited. You do get people who say they listen religiously, and since it's a Saturday I can only assume I've been doing inadvertent outreach, although the membership figures in my congregation don't show any blips (on the other hand, I haven't been there to see any). More than likely, they also go to church on Sunday, thus making for a very full weekend. Jews, of course, can't listen religiously (although the Reform can play the organ), once, again, because it's Saturday, although I do preach to the choir *après shabbos* in many communities—check your local times and listings. While I hate to bring it up in front of the *goyim,* with the Jewish male fan, typically an attorney (and a darned good one), you do run into the "anything Jew can do I can Jew better" attitude, when, frankly, they ought to stick to torts. If your closing arguments inspire rim shots from the court recorder, maybe you do have something going. Occasionally a personal injury man will break out of the pack for a show business career, but probably less often than truck drivers or bread van men. I guess it's the delivery.

Psychologically, the need for fans is obviously deep-seated and alarming when unmet, but it also is a high-wire act; people remember the Wallendas most from the time they flew. Fans know they can unmake you—maybe they tire of a relationship they don't see going anywhere. Guys must grow weary of hearing "Michael Feldman this, Michael Feldman that." Often they have expectations that can be confining: I remember somebody calling in during my radio stint at Dolly's (Fine Foods) who said, "You're really screwed up and unprofessional—don't ever change!" You do need to give something back to the fan since, after a while, the rain caps and wooden nickels don't appease them. Early on, I decided I would be the Tammy Wynette of public radio and always go out of my way to let my fans know that they had made me what I am today, even though they might have done a better job had they worked a little harder at it. After a show, I continue to sign autographs long after the crowd has gone. I know that somewhere out there, maybe not now, but soon, a kid will show up who's a little faster and a touch more freely associative, and who speaks more to the present time, but, darn it, Nora, I'm not ready to give it up just yet.

30

This Is Television

It was Chicago in August or Hell anytime. It was both the heat and the humidity. It was a chance to broadcast from Oprah Winfrey's studio at the least desirable time: when Oprah wasn't in it. Meanwhile, at the Michigan Avenue Hyatt, hotelier to the '68 convention disorders, Shriners mixing metaphors in fezzes and kilts played bagpipes in the atrium, sending shivers up the stand pipes until the very toilet water on the sixty-fourth floor tingled with excitement, which made one of us. I finessed a blotch on my nose with a dab of liquid makeup filched from my wife: war paint, for this was television.

Unlike the nose, the scenario was not rosy. I tried not to take the fact they hadn't had a room for me, the Michael Feldman of *Michael Feldman's Whad'ya Know?,* as a portent, but it was salt in the wound still festering after those fluorescent pink T-shirts appeared on the crew with me omitted or, maybe, tucked in, all aggravated by the disappearance of the fruit basket from the room and what sounded like the instantaneous assimilation of the executive producer, a

Pacific Palisades Jew, who no longer bothered to rub me the wrong way in a Yiddish accent.

Foot up on the camera dolly, the producer, still aglow from the last Jane Fonda workout video (low-impact) ever attempted, was scratching his salt and pepper in what I had come to recognize as an imitation-of-thought gesture. We had not been on the best of terms since I (humorously) suggested that while he was here in the Hog-butcher to the World, he do the top six buttons of his Melrose jungle print blouse or at least swap out the viewfinder around his neck for an Italian horn (had I known at the time that he was from Cincinnati and it couldn't be helped, I would have bit my tongue).

"How are you feeling?" he didn't really ask and, without waiting for me to try and frame the pall that had of late descended on me in the most positive light available, hit the ground running:

"Great. Just a few things. The monologue was terrific, but it's out—a time thing—you'll still have a minute at the top to introduce the band, explain the quiz, whatever you want to do with it. The audience interaction was a riot, but let's try it off-camera, before we roll, so we start up to speed. According to the focus group, we're getting tune-out there. You need to look into the camera more, and with your eyes open. . . . I know the lights are bright, but try not to squint. Plus, let's give the hair retoucher a try."

"Hair retoucher?" I said, snapping to. "You mean bald spot paint? The stuff in *The Fabulous Baker Boys*? Can't you just lose the crane shot?"

"Need it for the wide shots. You looked very sharp in the suit, but don't give your jacket to an audience member again; you've got all kinds of wires hanging down."

"But she was cold."

"We'll turn down the AC—Oprah likes it up. Sorry about the floor; I was really pissed they waxed it. The skating bit with the audience woman was nice, though; too bad we couldn't use it. The main thing is to make the spontaneity happen. It's not happening quickly enough."

"Tune out?" He nodded. "And Benito's in the green room."

Benito Schoenbaum, the studio exec, fused the best of both heritages: he was an extremely thoughtful man who could have you killed. His assistant, a ringer for Joan Lunden in a fog, brought in the sheaves of notes she took, he took, everybody took-took, exhuming one ream from the pile on her lap.

"I think we ought to drop the liposuction segment," she said. "Too graphic." Realizing she had mistakenly pulled the notes from the daytime surgical talk show they were shooting in Seattle (*Post Op:* during invasive surgery, the patient, under a local, fields questions from a live studio audience), she regrouped, while Benito laid the cold steel shibboleth against my temple.

"It's going well. A few things. The quiz is taking too long. The questions need to be easier."

"I could start with the answers," I replied, determined to use my wit to my disadvantage off air, too.

"Announcer: we might try it with a female, young black or Hispanic, or ideally all four."

"You want me to kill the old Norwegian male? He works on radio."

"The suit doesn't work for me."

"Me, neither. People know I don't have shoulders."

"Sweaters, maybe."

"I'll look like that guy in the infomercial."

"We did that."

"Chippendale dancers," "Joan" chipped in with what in any other business would have been a non sequitur, or maybe a recovered memory.

"Worked for Rick Dees," I said, incisively alluding to the disaster of the latest radio type to undergo TV humiliation.

"But he didn't have them playing a quiz," she countered. "You could have a lot of fun with them."

"Barrels. Do I dance with them, or just stick the used questions in their straps?"

"Try it both ways," she suggested. "Have fun with it."

"For the second quiz," Benito thought aloud, "what about a pair of female twins? Fantasy time for eighteen- to twenty-five-year-old males."

"I could have a lot of fun with them?"

"Exactly. And it works for the time slot."

"You don't think we're losing some of the things—the audience participation angle, the hominess, the 'you never know what will happen' feel—that people seem to like on radio?"

"This," they said in unison, "is television."

Being the trooper I am, I went out there and broke a leg. They had buffed the floor again. I'd like to tell you the Doublemint twins and I lived happily ever after, but the truth is I may never know pure chewing satisfaction and, to this day, do not attract eighteen- to twenty-five-year-old males.

IV

Because I Live Here

31

Coin of Our Realm

Two hundred fifteen thousand two hundred and seventy-three Wisconsinites have voted online just in two and a half days to pick our 2004 commemorative quarter design from three sifted and winnowed possibilities—the Wisconsin trinity: cow, corn, and cheese; a deer (exhibiting rather strange behavior, which could be the wasting or maybe it's just that he's never been with a muskie); and a fur trapper looking to screw an Indian out of a canoe-load of pelts. We won't know how it will all turn out for a couple of tension-packed days, but at least we managed to avoid the obvious. One entry had a Holstein head in three-quarter view, but I would have preferred the full profile, like Washington on the obverse, only pointing the other way so people know it's tails (if the Mint let you play around with it a little, a rump-on shot with tail rising would get a lot of laughs at the tavern, which is, after all, where all these things will be fed into the pull-tab machines). The Mint won't let you do U.S. currency in Colby orange, like our legend-dairy license plates were, which might make ours stand out from the rank-and-file of state quarters out there in a crowded field. Hopefully, there's nothing on any of our entries that will collapse and cause the state embarrassment, like the untimely passing of New Hampshire's Old Man of the Mountain, and nothing perceived as disjointed as Minnesota's attempt to put 10,000 lakes, the Star of the North, and a Viking ship racing a river boat to the Twin Cities, where natives making no appreciable gestures line the banks in greeting. I doubt that it happened that way. At least Wisconsin didn't try to cram it all in there and put cow, corn, cheese, deer, muskie, trapper, Indian, and canoe all on one quarter. That's too much pluribus for one unum.

Michigan had a lot of gall claiming all the great lakes on its quarter, I think; given the background that (1) Lake Michigan could be just as accurately called Lake Wisconsin, since its outline is just as much our inline as Michigan's (although this is consistent with their choosing a state symbol, a wolverine, that is bigger than our badger) and (2) the Upper Peninsula, to which they had to build a bridge to even connect it with the LP, is, by natural right, ours, growing out from Phelps as it does. That's the history, but where does Michigan, "Great Lakes State" though it is, get to claim Superior, Ontario, Erie, Huron, the St. Lawrence Seaway, and possibly the Finger Lakes, as well? It's a water grab. Iowa, at least, stuck to its own turf, with a nice little Grant Wood of a little church-like school house, or a school-like church house, with either the schoolmarm or the pastor's wife outside with some of the incorrigibles on "pose for the quarter day." "Foundation in Education," don't you know. It's hard not to feel, as an outsider, that they missed a bet by voting the American Gothic couple off the coin (ideally, him on one side, her on the other), but they're probably pretty tired of that shit by now. Iowans don't really look like that anymore; well, kind of, but they smile. Well, it's their quarter. Probably the biggest of all missed opportunities, though, in all this state give-no-quarter madness, was Oregon's not stamping one of the designs proposed by artists for the

Portland Tribune: Tom McCall superimposed over the state with hand held palm out and the legend "Don't Even Visit," or the more traditional Meriwether Lewis standing next to "Pioneering Death with Dignity." One of those would have been a hoot. I don't know what we could have done for Wisconsin along the same lines, maybe "Free Highways" (a slap at Illinois) or a glass of milk with those rising sun rays so popular in numismatics behind it and the legend, à la "Live Free or Die," "Lactose Tolerance."

It may be we missed a chance to tell people something they didn't know about Wisconsin. They seem to know about the cows, even though we tried to keep them quiet. Cows are nice animals, or 4H kids wouldn't sleep with them in their stalls at the State Fair, but Wisconsin is a lot more than cows, God bless 'em. Machine parts, for example; although it's hard to put a machine part on a coin and have people know what it is or does, particularly with all the solid-state components these days. Going with the time-honored gear-and-cog motif, you get the Rotary but alienate the Kiwanis and the Knights of Columbus. Precision instruments are made here, but not everyone wants a Johnson Control in his pants pocket. Beer we don't make so much of, anymore, but we still consume it as if we did, so there's some logic in the Wisconsin obverse just saying "Good for One Large Drink." Paper products, well, maybe if they give us a shot at the folding money; it probably should be perforated, anyway. Many of the nation's largest insurers are headquartered in Wisconsin—American Family, Sentry, Wausau—one could easily envision an underwriter in full stride, briefcase swinging, within the outline of the state, sort of like Illinois did with Lincoln, although they have a better shape to work with, particularly with long, tall Abe. To fit in our mitten we'd need a short, former wrestler type of agent, which, fortunately, most of them have to be to get anywhere at it. Maybe a competition encouraging artists to depict a preexisting condition or act of God would have produced some results suitable for the coin of our realm.

32

The Midwest

Where Is It?

Recent survey results suggest that most people don't know where the Midwest is, including many who live there (or would, if they only knew where they were). Asked which states make up the American Midwest, respondents to a national poll could agree on only one: Iowa. But Iowa does not exist in a vacuum. "Are we not hog producers, too?" asks Wisconsin. "Do our whitefish cheeks not taste as sweet?" cries Minnesota. "Where do you think the corn palace is?" pipes up South Dakota.

Still, it's easy to be confused, even living here. In Wisconsin, we regularly get tossed into the Great Lakes States or tagged with the glamorous sobriquet the Upper Midwest. Occasionally we're just asked to check "glaciated" or "non-" (Milwaukee being the Queen City of glacier till, the place where even the Ice Age stopped). Territorial integrity has been hard to come by: our doppelganger,

Minnesota, is often mistakenly listed in atlases among "States, Scandinavian" (if that is a mistake; I mean, what's really the difference between a finger lake and a fjord?), while Canadians think they can walk right on into North Dakota (where the border patrol has been less than vigilant) in spite of the insidious Canadian knack for blending in right up until they say "aboot," by which time it is often too late.

If, in fact, there is no Midwest (except Iowa), we have another potential Balkan situation on our hands to be resolved at an international conference in Dayton, even though Ohio is part of the problem—is it east? Is it west? What about Toledo? Then there is the always perplexing Indiana—hobnobbing with Easterners, lilting like Southerners—and yet accredited by *Midwest Living* magazine (that's right, published in Des Moines) as one of the twelve constituent states entitled to subscribe, along with Illinois (which, around Carbondale, most resembles West Virginia), Kansas (Great Plains, anyone?), Michigan (half of which sets its clocks to New York City time, thank you), Missouri (the Gateway to all four major directions), Nebraska (loaded with Heartland values, but, excuse me, aren't those buffalo?), and the aforementioned North and South Dakotas, Ohio, Wisconsin, Minnesota, and the nucleus around which we all spin—Iowa.

Historically, much of the confusion regarding the exact location of the Midwest stems from the relative nature of terms like "mid" and "west," the legacy of the congressionally declaimed Northwest Territory, which, veneer stripped away, turns out to look a lot like Ohio or perhaps "Ohioland," as in "The Greater Ohioland Ford Dealers." Today, many of us (with no particular ax to grind; I've had some good times in Ohio) would place Ohio in the East, at least as far as Columbus (and we'd concede that as well if it meant the Wisconsin Badgers never had to play at Ohio State again). To refresh your seventh-grade memory, the Northwest Territory was the region north of the Ohio River and east of the Mississippi, constituting what today we think of as the heart of the Midwest (minus Iowa!); had the nation rested on its laurels in 1787, the Midwest would be the home of Starbucks coffee, and Bill Gates's high-tech hacienda would be carved out of a bluff in South Beloit. The Northwest Territory is not to be confused with the Northwest Territories, encompassing Baffin Island and everything else that couldn't be conveniently stuffed into Canada, or with the Northwest Frontier in Pakistan. The rule of thumb is if Punjab is to the right and Peshawar is to the left, you are no longer in the Midwest and should call AAA immediately.

As America pushed willy-nilly westward toward its date with Manifest Destiny, it acquired another Northwest entirely, carelessly flinging aside the former and still perfectly good one, leaving it just a little hurt as well as up for grabs geopolitically. Congress never bothered to incorporate the Midwest Territories; if Lewis and Clark ever came through these parts, they didn't mention it. To this day, the Midwest, which performs a great service to the nation by keeping New York and Los Angeles apart, is disparaged as the Fly-Over States by jet-setting bicoastals who would do well not to forget whose air space they're crossing (namely the Midwestern home of the Strategic Air Command). In fact, the Midwest (and here I'm assuming we do exist) is the only region of the nation that came into being as a convenient place to store values: the Heartland, full of hardworking, religious but not overly zealous, family-oriented, parka-wearing (one for everyday, one for Sunday), tolerant, helpful folk who fall into two main categories: links and patties. Since the bulk of such people (no pun intended; many of us are large-boned) seem to fall in the midst of the country (once grits are served automatically at breakfast and seed caps yield to Texas T's, you've gone too far), the area they gravitated to came to be known as the Middle West, or, in racier modern parlance, the Midwest.

Which brings us back to the initial question: where is it? Here's a little experiment you can try at home, using an ordinary atlas opened to the United States. You'll notice that the crease runs right through Fargo, Sioux Falls, Wichita, and Dallas—let this be the "Y" axis. Now, if you lean on the map, you'll see San Francisco, Denver, Kansas City, Cincinnati, and Norfolk running along the top of your forearm. Let this be the "X" axis. The point at which your forearm intersects with the crease would therefore be the center of the nation, or a spot about equidistant between Beatrice and Peru, Nebraska—let's call it Elk Creek, because they'll probably enjoy the attention. Now, removing your glasses, place the tip of your nose directly on Elk Creek and, if your eyesight is anything like mine, everything you will be able to read on the map without moving your head will be the Midwest—Nebraska, South Dakota, enough of North Dakota to count them in, Kansas, Minnesota, Iowa, Missouri, Wisconsin, Illinois, Indiana up to about Kokomo, and, if you really furl your brow, Kalamazoo, Michigan. (I can't for the life of me make out Ohio, but no system is perfect. If they say they are, then they are.)

Since this coincides with the commonly accepted notion of the dominion of the Midwest without having to resort to cumbersome demographics, average household incomes, or predominance of heavy-equipment manufacturing or number of acres in soybeans, and since it is consistent with a good deal of anecdotal evidence gathered from people who claim to be from around here, this then would appear to be the Midwest. Please commit it to memory; if there's still some doubt, please write for directions.

33

Moo-Yah!

An Editorial

Not content with merely driving their fancy foreign cars through our fair state at speeds approaching that of light, our flatland friends to the south have devised a new and more ominous violation of the Badger sovereignty—a 4,000-foot long atomic shotgun Saddam Hussein would have died for that will plow a subatomic furrow of neutrinos through our productive loam all the way from Janesville to Superior. The Fermilab people (you know, where the buffalo roam atop the nuclear particle accelerator) have decided that the shortest distance between Batavia, Illinois, and Soudan, Minnesota, is a diagonal across Wisconsin, where any particles that haven't been absorbed by our indigenous population of pets and livestock will plink on a massive detector plate sunk in an iron mine. The 450-mile trip will take the muon (yes, that's right, moo-on; the joke's not lost on us) neutrinos 2.5 milliseconds, something to shoot for the next time a commodities broker nonstops it from Barrington to Tomah in the Quattro Sport Turbo. The object: to find out if neutrinos have any mass. If they don't, fine, they'll pass through us like light through yon window; if they do—we're talking entry wound in Sharon and exit in Superior.

While in Illinois they will impale nothing bigger than South Elgin, in Wisconsin muons will initially pierce Sharon and then proceed to skewer Allen's Grove, Janesville, Milton, Lake Koshkonong, Sun Prairie, Delores, Arlington, Poynette, the junction of 90/94 and 51/39 during the height of the Dells' tourist season, Briggsville, and Easton, taking Adams and sparing Friendship, string Dellwood, New Miner, Babcock, Lindsey, Chili, Loyal, Longwood, Withee, Lublin, Gilman, Donald, Sheldon, Conrath, Ladysmith, and Exeland like beads, spear the fiberglass muskie at Hayward, Solon Springs, and Bennett, take out Superior and spare co-conspirator Duluth (Minnesota being in collusion on this thing), and skip like a stone over Fish Lake before smacking the lead plate in Soudan.

Illinois is a good long state; they could point the thing at Cairo, still get in their 450 miles, and keep all the credit in state. Couldn't they point it straight up and wear lead sombreros? Couldn't they ask before we have to read about it in the Chicago papers where the map insert shows the familiar outline of our beloved state with a slash through it labeled "muon path"? As I figure it, 4 trillion neutrinos a second times ten years, the life of the project, is a lot of neutrinos passing under the very hoofs of Holsteins already suffering from the effects of stray voltage and cell phones. At the very least, some of the $136 million could be earmarked as payments for right of way—otherwise, I'll bet there's more than one sheet metal guy in Walworth County who'd be only too happy to jury-rig our own preemptive massive deflector on our side of Highway 67.

Maybe we should talk.

34

Minnesota Man Fakes Death

They jailed the Minnesota man who faked his death. You've got to wonder why they would single out one from so many. Drive through New Ulm alone, and you'll see 13,594 you had no idea were thriving under the Hermann (the German) Mausoleum that dominates the town; stop at Happy Joe's and you'll infer the burghers are indeed alive, if not kicking. On our side, we're not immune to this kind of thing: there was a state legislator from Wisconsin years ago who faked his death in a boating accident (when they found the case of Old Milwaukee untouched in the cooler, they knew something was horribly wrong), the body eventually washing through the St. Lawrence and down the Atlantic coast to the Bahamas, where state funds awaited offshore; it worked for a while until his Packer gear gave him away.

Those of us busy trying to fake a life look at a story like this and wonder how it works, and if it might work for us. The appeal of closing your books without going through probate on the one hand

and being your own beneficiary on the other is hard to deny (the gentleman here was uninsured; I'm just thinking out loud), although it might be easier trying to cash out the disability insurance (which they get an arm and a leg for) what with the redundancy of so many of our organs and extremities. Short of being mainland Irish and having your buddies take your stiff pub crawling until they don't know which of you to bury, faking your death would be the next best thing to being there, and you could send for the guys later.

The deceased, fifty, of St. Paul, was unusually enterprising in faking a heart attack immediately upon being pulled over by a state trooper for inattentive driving and in following up the performance (which trooper Glen Knippenberg said he didn't believe for a minute, but there was no emergency acting squad to call) with a glowing review in the *St. Paul Pioneer Press* obits that included the accolade(s) "Loved by everyone: loved everyone" and the obligatory yearbook picture from 1979 showing him so young and so not dead. (The paper said they always verify deaths with funeral homes, but this, being a private service, slipped through the cracks, along with payment for the notice.) No sarcophagus or casket—thrifty stock, these—merely a fax from the next world to the judge in this one from a Mr. Isabella, AAL (attorney at law? Aid Association for Lutherans?) noting his client's untimely passing (from the Office Max in Maplewood—a critical mistake) and suggesting that his open cases with the county could now be shut—and "thanks for your time." The Washington County District Court judge, believing in the here and now in the great Minnesota free-thinking tradition, merely added the fax to the court file, already bulging with charges of felony assault (from the flailing during the Fred Sanford imitation), legal if not coronary obstruction, and driving with a license he owed them at least corneas and kidneys on. If he had been smart, he would've donated something.

Life after death reportedly looks a lot like the Washington County Jail, with limbo, a $10,000 bond, and a lot of time to think about loving, and being loved.

35

(Still) One Big Individual

Thirty-eight acres of fungus would seem to be more than enough, but it pales in comparison to 2,385 and growing. Ever since that day in the UP (the Upper Peninsula of Michigan) around Crystal Falls when somebody pulled and pulled and the *Armillaria mellea*—honey mushroom—wouldn't come up, the folks in Crystal Falls have known they were onto something. To their credit, they parlayed the 38-acre mushroom into a Letterman Top Ten list topped by "Bill Clinton once tried to smoke some of it," before interest (and the President) flagged.

National attention is a fickle thing, but Crystal Falls has managed to stretch out its fifteen minutes of fame with fungus tours, fungus paraphernalia, and, of course, Humongous Fungus Fest, usually held the second week of August, "Tons of Fun" being the theme last year, with the parade up Superior Avenue featuring woodsy floats with Forest Park grade-schoolers dressed as button mushrooms and throwing tendrils to the crowd while the Lion's Band plays and the crowd's attention is riveted by the release of the 1,500 lucky plastic mushrooms (at two bucks a cap) over the Paint River Bridge. You can win $500, which still leaves $2,500 unaccounted for. The good people of Crystal Falls have done much to combat the stereotype of the common root rot fungus by creating a little excitement around it with the mini–draft horse pull, the Finn-versus-Polack ethnic softball championship at Runkle Park, a teen dance with DJ (after getting all worked up from the parade, maybe not a good idea), the buckboard and horseshoe tourneys, the world's largest mushroom pizza, baked by the Lions, all this capped, following the pie social and the academic boosters pasty (call if you need this explained) sale at the United Methodist and the First National parking lots, respectively, by the mother of all flea markets, covering most of the 2,000-year-old-plus subterranean growth with "anything from crafts to rummage." That some rhizomorphs creep under the border to the Wisconsin side makes the world's largest living organism not a little source of local pride in Presque Isle, on the Wisconsin side of things, where we have learned not to grudge Yoopers (as they are said to call themselves) anything they can feel good about.

Just when, from out of the musk, comes word of a 9.65-square-kilometer (2,385-acre agribusiness size) *Armillaria ostoyae* that could cover 1,600 football fields should the need ever arise, and until then most of the Malheur National Forest in Oregon. Forget for a moment that the mushrooms of this species, scaly brown things up to a foot across with a brownish annulus, can cause gastronomical upset (due, one expert thinks, to overeating), forget that their cellulose fangs are sucking the lifeblood out of what is nearly the last stands of virgin giant conifers in the northwest—we'll not see stands of virgins like these again—or that the huge wartlike rings of mycelium that blanket the forest floor make it look like the world's largest skin disease, and consider the impact—economic, social, political, psychological—on the UP and on Yoopers. I'm not saying that it's third world up there, but when you've got to go to Eagle River for action, you know things can get slow. Ontonagon has the ski hills; Crystal Falls has the fungus.

I checked, and although the Malheur Forest area offers an impressive number of year-round events—the Ducks Unlimited and Wild Turkey Foundation banquets, the Seneca Handicap Trap Shoot and Grant County Snowballers, the gun and sports expo and motorcycle rally at the fairgrounds, the quilt-ins, re-enactments, and fly-ins, the Christmas meat trap shoot—none of them, not one, is *Armarillia* related, zero-mushroom themed, and nothing noted on the sign into town. The only novelty ceramic salt and pepper shakers you'll find are the breast ones you see all over. You've got to ask somebody in Corvallis even where it is; perhaps you'll get the same individual who determined that this was, in fact, one individual and not a collective of like-minded root rotters; in no way does it come close to what Mellea (some call her Bulbosa, some just "Honey") is to Crystal Falls, namely the largest employer outside of Krist Oil (actually in Iron Mountain).

I'm not sure what can be done. There is some hope that spore testing will prove the Eastern Oregon organism to be the Eastern Oregon organism*s,* some that the whole thing will blow over once the flurry of press releases and studies of implications for the Canadian lumber industry stop and the gaze of mycologists and thrill seekers alike will fall back to the teeming soil around Crystal Falls, the Jewel in the Crown of the UP, where there are still openings in the Industrial Park, an official Michigan renaissance zone (no tax-free liquor, but other advantages—inquire). Regardless of what happens, there can be no question that Mellea, while perhaps not the biggest, is one very big individual—from the air she resembles a giant mushroom cap that, once on the ground again, turns out to be almost exactly the weight of a giant blue whale, if you could pull it out. One big individual well worth the seeing.

36

Mourning Becomes DuWayne

I don't know about you, but there are mornings when I wake up wanting nothing more than to blast a bird of peace, particularly if one's been cooing outside my window since six. Now I have my chance: the Mourning Dove Hunt is joined. There was some controversy regarding shooting the Official State Bird of Peace, but it ran up against another Wisconsin imperative, formulated recently as a constitutional amendment: the natural right to hunt just about anything not on a leash, a.k.a. the Compulsory Hunting Law. There is strong sentiment in the Badger State for making everybody report to deer camp for basic training in the hunting arts, including muzzle loading (your own and that of your weapons), disassembling and reassembling your weapon while blind from drink, banging the bar dice for a while at the Tomahawk while considering strategy, and making at least a good-faith effort to get up in the tree stand. Many proponents in the state felt that the amendment was necessary because the U.S.

165

Constitution's Second Amendment, since it doesn't specifically mention 12-gauge shotguns, is soft on hunting.

The *Zenaida macroura* is good hunting, in that they don't move
much while you reload, although some enthusiasts claim they zigzag
(possibly a reaction to their enthusiasm). They already harvest them
by the foot locker in a lot of places, most notably Texas, where the
One-Armed Dove Shoot in Olney is legendary and has particular
appeal in that one-armed guys shoot the birds and two-armed guys
have to fetch 'em. Around here we're just happy to be able to cull the
critters, no matter our particular physical challenge. Feelings run
high: 27,000 citizens turned out last year for a Natural Resources
Board meeting (which usually draws as many as 37), 22,000 of
whom voted to waste the flying rats, with Rep. DuWayne Johnsrud
leading the charge against the admittedly not very hard-to-take
dove, going so far as to fricassee a mess of them in his capitol office
(there were noticeably fewer pigeons on the porticos that week) and
offer tiny little drumsticks to all takers. Tastewise, they are said to
run somewhat to the crow side of squab, but as the French (who pop
those little birds of theirs whole) say, *la sauce est toute.* They run only
about five ounces, so you've got to eat a lot of them. As Johnsrud
notes, "There are those people out there who don't want you to eat
anything that's got a face on it," which, apparently, is not as reason-
able as it sounds. If you ever see anyone with a face like a mourning
dove you probably want to leave what's in your glass and head out
the door (since it may be an avatar), but his point is well taken. Personally, I will not eat anything with glasses.

The mourning dove season runs from September through late
October, with a limit of fifteen winged things with faces on them per
hunter per day. They should last a while, although it's worth noting
that Wisconsin once had the largest nestings of passenger pigeons
anywhere; at their peak, in 1871, they packed some 850 square miles
at one sitting—an estimated 136 million birds, all of which were

shipped out in barrels in boxcars heading for the garment centers of the nation for ladies' hats. The last was shot by a conservationist in 1899, making the woods safe, once again, for berries. If dove shooting once again becomes the rage, mourning may become DuWayne Johnsrud.

37

Mad-Is-One

The whooping cranes have Baraboo, home of the Crane Foundation, and me, I have Madison, just to the south as the sandhill flies. Without Madison I'd be a couple of years shy of retiring from teaching, having long since resigned myself to starting class by saying, "Turn to page 234 . . ." and knowing the kids were waiting me out until the sleep disorder kicked in (we had a teacher like that back at Washington High in Milwaukee—taught Social Slumbers). Were Madison a figment of my imagination and nothing more, my life would have been (radically) different: I wouldn't have gotten the (intermittent, since we shut down the u so often) education I got, wouldn't have met either of the wives, and wouldn't be on the radio, most likely, at least with the American Motors show no longer on in WLIP in Kenosha. Regardless, I still like it here. It appears to be my natural environment.

And I'm not the only one. A lot of us would simply not be us elsewhere, or maybe we'd be us, but we'd be few and far between. A lot of places would neither celebrate our diversity, have us envision whirled peas, or encourage us to question authority, which, admittedly, was more of a priority before the authority was us. While not quite the escape from reality purported, Madison is not exactly a headlong rush toward it, either. To think of it as merely the anti-Beloit is neither accurate nor fair to Beloit; Madison is in Wisconsin but not of it; we have the largest lesbian zip code anywhere (53704); per capita, more people read the *New York Times* here than in Manhattan; and hardly anyone between Sun Prairie and Middleton eats within his or her own birth culture. Ethnicity is by choice. We have no need for the term "alternative lifestyle" as used on the outside, and "same-sex couple" is redundant. The 10 Percent Society, here, is hetero, while the La Leche League is engorged. Nontraditional healers leave no bezoars unturned. The yellow bicycles are for anyone to use. Gender is optional. Yes, we have those little radios, and anything goes, but it's a far cry from the popular myth (north of Highway 29) that, eventually, the aliens will return for us and fly the capitol dome back to a midsize, highly livable planet somewhere on Orion's belt—even though that's how far you'd have to go to find another Madison, and then it wouldn't be the same.

Not that the times here they are not a changin'. Once the forge where leftist firebrands were plunged, if that's what you do in a forge, Madison today only aids and comforts my friend Karl Armstrong, the last living Wisconsin radical, who runs a very successful deli (Radical Rye) after, for many years, selling Angela Davis smoothies from a cart on the mall. What a country, Madison! Along with his brother Dwight, driving a cab again after the microscopy thing didn't pan out, these two are All-American City boys here. Alan Ruff, a Groucho Marxist, still turns up, but the Moonies don't come through any more for him to heckle. They must be divorcing strangers in mass ceremonies these days. I do miss Wayne the hellfire preacher with the oxfords who used to come and call us "Wisconsin," along with his befuddled girlfriend, "cyn-di." Simon Sparrow, whose painting was a lot more lighthearted than his preaching, died years ago, and his "primitive" art is worth a civilized fortune. You don't hear about the guy living in the steam tunnels, coming up only to shower in the library sinks, anymore; I hope he's okay. I still see the guy who used to spit on important people; I think he's still spitting, although I doubt the gobs he used to hack up. They took all of the hookahs and pipes out of the Pipefitter, not that I would have noticed, and now sell just boxing nuns and novelties. The 602 Club is long gone, green walls and pickled eggs and all—there is no longer any place in Madison where you can sit in a booth, play hearts, and push a doorbell for a beer. Dolly's Fine Food (where I did my first radio show) and Dolly are no more, and the Mickey's on Williamson no longer sports the fetal deer tableau over the bar, probably because the taxidermist across the street is now a pizza parlor. Our former radical mayor is a financial adviser these days, a business that was going so well he even ran for mayor again, just for the cash flow. While Eddie Ben-Elson is no longer with us, they still put his sunken Planet of the Apes Statue of Liberty out on the ice every winter; just daring Charlton Heston to come by and scream, "God damn you all!" which, around here, he would have a variety of reasons for saying.

Despite what you've heard about the University of Wisconsin, it is currently a hotbed of student rest (although that might be mono), subject to change should the draft come back. "Draft Beer, Not Students" would resound with the class of 2004. The outside agitators all seem to be on the inside now and have been ever since the New York and Chicago grads came back to buy all the previously ridiculously cheap housing out from under us locals. Driven out by targeted tuition increases to punish them for causing the '60s, they own the early years of this millennium. Other than that, a lot of the kids from my graduating class, the highly abbreviated class of '70 (we could choose pass or fail; I chose "pass"), are coming back to retire in condos with Lake Mendota views, possibly not even realizing these are dorm conversions and that, in fact, the one they paid big bucks for is the same place where what's-her-name with hair down to her ass, the one who practiced Kundalini, used to live. Well, Karma and Carmex, that's Madison. I was here when all the guys on Bassett, Broom, and Dayton posted their draft lottery numbers in the window; one guy right on the southeast corner of Broom and West Washington had 11 in the window; it was there long after he split for either Canada or the service. Mine said "354": more Madison luck.

V

Feldmanity

38

My Manhood

When I grow up I'm going to be a scientist with my own observatory a giant telescope, chemicals, and other things. My observatory is going to be like Mt. Wilsons. I am going to have a special lab. In it I am going to have microscopes, test tubes and an electric eye to open the door. Michael Feldman

My manhood didn't turn out the way I thought it would, but whose does ? Steve Walder, who was on the same page of Mrs. Bubrick's *When I Grow Up* book (Jay, her son and my best friend at Sherman School until he started to run with Ricky Dominitz and his crowd, gave me a Xerox a few years ago), said he wanted to be a football player "or even a baseball player"; whether he ever became a catcher and caught "speed balls, spit balls, or even ko-ko balls," I don't know if he succeeded, and I haven't come across a "ko-ko" ball, either. I haven't heard of him professionally, unless he played under another name (not that there's anything wrong with "Steve Walder"), but it's not like I've followed every sport at every level. He had good power, I remember, while being somewhat lumbering on the base paths and in his oral reports.

Of course, I'm no rocket scientist, either. I know what happened—when I finally learned—must have been in ninth-grade biology—what the scientific method involved, all that rigor-mortis soon set in and I knew it was more work than I wanted to do (not realizing, then, that you could fake your results and still make a good living) and gave up on the dream. I feel like I let down the spirit of International Geophysical Year, promoted extensively by *My Weekly Reader* in 1957, the year of Sputnik, and, for some reason never fully explained, the world's deepest hole, Moho. What a great name for a hole. My description of my future was pretty much what Arthur was already doing in our basement in his science lab (formerly Howard's sports room—from which, he claims, I copped his Ted Williams letter and collection of vintage baseball cards and gave them [ironically] to the same Jay Bubrick who turns out to be integral in my personal history, all of which Jay categorically denies and I just can't remember. Mom probably threw them all out, along with all my good stuff.).

Arthur had what was, for the time and the basement, a state-of-the-art lab, having run a hose from the stove downstairs to the Bunsen burner on his bench, explaining why his mother was always smelling gas she could never find the source of, and converted Uncle Max's highboy humidor into a airless bell chamber, to what end I (fortunately) never found out. After Jeffrey Dahmer, naturally, we had to rethink what went on there, but we couldn't tie Arthur to any disappearances other than his own, every night. I think it was pure science. Arthur had a centrifuge before it was fashionable, even though it was made from a record turntable going 78 rpm, and what he claimed was an atomic clock running on the radium that used to come in Chemcraft sets. He euthanized insects and small mammals alike, painlessly, with chloroform; bled himself onto slides, looking, perhaps, for a clue about himself none of us upstairs had, either; reassembled mice from parts in regurgitated owl pellets; grafted plants to animals or, possibly, the other way around; had specimens to die for floating in jars of formaldehyde; and even practiced a kind of alchemy, trying to convert lead (gathered from wheel weights gleaned from the rims of Uptown Motors cream puffs) into Arthurium, an element found only in his nature. On a good day, he'd let you play with his mercury, recovered from our thermometers; on a bad day, he wouldn't let you watch him attempt to make synthetic diamonds from briquettes. If it's rocks you were after, Art had 'em: sedimentary, conglomerate, schist, fool's gold (guess who was the fool?), your feldspars, your quartzes, your rare earths; he had trilobites and stalactites and a beer bottle melted from lightning from Bradford beach. Downstairs, Erector set robots did Arthur's bidding. The famous birdshit butterfly, the only birdshit ever to fly on its own power, was on display, as well as a meteorite, looking suspiciously like furnace slag, that Arthur believed contained alien seed pods, or so he told me. Most days, he wouldn't allow me anywhere near his research, always in a critical stage, while others, he actually let me kill a few things or hold my hand over the x-ray tube that I don't think, strictly speaking, he should have had. I admired his scientific bent, especially when I learned that, if I simply lowered my horizon, his homemade reflecting celestial telescope could help me observe Shelly Walkimer, across the street, astronomically. You think the guys at Mt. Wilson never lower their sights?

My unrealized manhood—not fully stated in the Bubrick document—was to share a bachelor duplex pad with my pal Teddy Simning, who also wanted to be a scientist, or at least was willing to when I explained the perks: lab assistants! The key feature of our swinging Scienceplex would be the electric-eye door—like the one at the National T, much better than the mat you had to jump on repeatedly at the A&P to get the door to open and close repeatedly. Whatever the future might be, it seemed certain that breaking the beam of an electric eye would open it. Ronald Reagan, the host of *General Electric Theater* after the Old Ranger croaked, had them in his all-electric gold medallion house. Like Arthur, although not in degree, I had a lot of applied-tech ideas crowding my brain, like a screw-in fluorescent tube (long before they became available), unfortunately three feet long on the drawing board and thus hard to screw in, and auto headlights that got brighter as you sped up so you'd never out-drive your lights again, although the number of oncoming drivers blinded probably would be a net safety loss. Atomic piles in the home were *Popular Science*'s and not my idea, but I was a big proponent of 'em and pneumatic tubes, like the ones that sucked orders around in Schuster's, thinking they might one day whisk my mother to Schuster's without the need of a fossil-fuel-consuming bus. As for tangible results, though, it pretty much came down to bomb making, rather a typical stage in the presexual boy of my day. If you could convince them at the drug store that your mom wanted some saltpeter to sprinkle on your food, you could use that, crush up some of Arthur's briquettes, throw in some sulfur from the chemistry set, and blow open any milk chute between Wauwatosa and Grant Boulevard. Once puberty struck, little explosions ensuing from another chemistry altogether preoccupied Teddy and me, and the pursuit of my manhood proceeded on a most unscientific basis.

39

1965

Nineteen sixty-five started out promisingly—I passed my driver's test on only the second try (Dad didn't exactly teach me to drive, and he certainly didn't cover parallel parking)—I was making a cool $1.50 an hour just for hiding in the stock room at Auto Parts & Service Company, the Beatles came out with *Rubber Soul,* and Dylan countered with *Highway 61 Revisited.* In the spring, Miss Ganos, my English teacher, talked me into taking part in Tonia Toppers, Washington High's annual variety show, where I wrote the skits, populated them with my friends, and got to be master of ceremonies in a tuxedo, no less, doing very nearly what I do today on the radio verbatim. My parents sat in the balcony; afterward, Dad was in the beaming stage, his highest accolade. Having done some emceeing of his own at odd Odd Fellows functions and sundry accounting awards ceremonies, Dad knew what it took.

In the fall, things went south; to Atlanta in the case of the Braves, after months of denial and much rending of garments and gnashing of teeth for Milwaukeeans. Granted, in the end they were drawing only a few thousand, but they had a team on which Bob Uecker was a starter. Today teams move so often nobody thinks baseball is much more than a shell game (which dome are they under?), but, if "Pride Builds Milwaukee" like they claimed on the sides of the garbage trucks (even those filling the tavern lots for lunch), this was a major hit to civic pride. A good baseball town, as the minor-league Brewers had proved, Milwaukee had stolen the Braves from Boston fair and square in 1952, and when they showed up with the rookie Henry Aaron, Eddie Mathews, Spahn, and Burdette, it felt like the Renaissance must have felt in Venice, I mean if you like paintings and such. Nobody didn't love the Braves. Dad used to get tickets from his larger clients—Afram Brothers, scrap metal, and the Basses, hoteliers—and I would take the bus over to the ballpark, scalp nine, and use one (good seats, too, lower grandstand, first base side, and, once in a while, boxes), sometimes spending a school day in County Stadium, the days a Braves game was considered a legitimate absence (you just had to get your ticket stamped in the office). The loss of the Braves was a blow to all of us; it was impossible to imagine Dad not sitting on the porch, smoke rising, listening to Earl Gillespe's play-by-play on the radio stuck in the window, even after the porch ranks had been thinned by Uncle Max's death during the 1960 season (the start of the Braves' decline after tying for, and losing, the pennant in '59).

In 1965, I got my first radio gigs, on WOKY and WRIT Milwaukee's two rock 'n' roll stations, having sent both the same entry for their on-air contests, which said I had acquired the elocution of a local Demosthenes by practicing speaking with pebbles in my mouth down at Bradford Beach. What can I say, I always had a flourish. After I played Tony Newley's "What Kind of Fool Am I?" for the Braves' general manager, Bob Barry (the Fifth Beatle; actually, the 15,000th) told me I was over the top. At WRIT, I played "Louie, Louie" and inferred the words; the station manager said I talked too much and should go to college and forget about radio, good advice that I attempted to take. Nineteen sixty-five was also the year Dad made me dump the girl I had asked to the prom and take instead Betty Jean Klipstein (not her real name) because he had met her father, a greengrocer, on the train to Blue Island (Slag and Smelting) and had confirmed that she was Jewish and in my class; unfortunately, he had neglected to confirm her psychiatric history. Fortunately, the girl I abandoned took it well, merely going with my best friend, Dick, and *putting out* at the post-prom, while Betty Jean pretended to fall asleep (a big dinner does that to you now, not then) on my arm in the parking ramp while I vainly tried to undo at least few dozen of the hundred, maybe a hundred twenty buttons on her grandmother's lace gown. What can I tell you, I was sixteen. I do remember, that summer, getting a little further with the girl next door while her parents were out of town and, after being cut short, bounding down her porch steps to find Dad standing on our lawn airing out his cigar; giving me a knowing smile as I squeaked a little "Hi, Dad!" It was well known, or at least imagined, that Dad had been a ladies' man in his day; Mother occasionally referred to The Redhead, who was just the last one he was engaged to before Mom (I used to play with his string of old engagement rings; apparently you got them back in those days). Mom, herself, was engaged to another man, Hilton Weiss, whom she dumped like a load of bricks when he wanted her to live with his mother.

My oldest brother, Clayton, told me that the worst thing he ever had to do in life, so far, happened in 1965, which was, while in the guise of a Marquette medical school student, assisting our family doctor (the chain-smoking) Dr. Saichek, in confirming the extent of Dad's prostate gland. Apparently, there's only one way to do this; it is the very reason the admonition against physicians examining family members exists. It certainly carries "dutiful son" too far (Clayton had already been sent into brothels and flophouses downtown as a teenager to attempt to collect for the ill-fated credit clothing store—Dad's partnership in Floyd's, where you could put $5 down and skip town in a new suit. Surgery, which by 1965 had advanced only slightly from trepanning, was indicated. Afterward, when I saw him in the hospital, Dad was ambulating the halls of Mt. Sinai like Diogenes with a catheter instead of a lamp, training to get back to fight the good accounting fight. "I'm in good shape for the shape I'm in," he said, not for the first time.

We'd been through this before. The reason I love lilacs is that the bushes that for years gamely tried to screen the alley abutting our house were in full bloom the day Dad came back from the hospital after his (second) stroke, the one during which Milwaukee's finest assumed he was driving unpowered on the shoulder of the East-West Freeway because he was a Milwaukeean. That time, he recovered fully, with accounting abilities intact, and I was grateful to the lilacs. Afterward, though, at ten, I developed the habit of watching him when he slept on the couch with the paper over his face to make sure the Green Sheet was rising and falling. Eventually, when I got my license, I could drive Dad to his medical appointments when he wasn't up to it, but, thank God, I wasn't in medical school, and no heroic procedures were asked of me.

Dad seemed to have bounced back again after this one; he said Dr. Saichek wanted to write up his surgery for the medical journal, it went so well. "Is it good to see your dad back in the swing of things?" he asked me when he got home. I said, "Dad, it's always good to see you, especially in the swing of things" (in that middle-aged way I've always had of phrasing things) and reached for my camera to take a picture of him with accounting ledgers under his arms like wings. The camera didn't flash. On that same night in October 1965, he wasn't feeling well; I heard him get up a couple of times and Mother fixing him Alka-Selzer, which, at the time, may have been an approved treatment for a coronary thrombosis. I didn't get up, though, one of the many things I blamed myself for years afterward. Before dawn, my mother yelled for me, and I came into their room to find Dad lying face down on the bed, breathing with difficulty, and Mother trying in vain to turn him over. In that weird calm that occurs when you're in shock, I at first methodically shuffled through my wallet trying to find my Red Cross lifesaver card, which illustrated mouth-to-mouth resuscitation, which I tried; Dad breathed his last breath into me and died in my arms. When the ambulance came, they took him out over the porch where we had sat and listened to Braves games, with the sheet pulled off his face as a courtesy. Mom went in the ambulance, and I drove Dad's '61 Impala ('61 had been only a Chevy year; Dad had a new '66 Olds on order, we found out later, so '66 should have been a good year) in circles through the streets of Wauwatosa, where the county hospital used to be, where my few driving miles had never taken me.

I cried for a lot of years, beginning in 1965. I should have talked to somebody about my grief and my guilt for letting Dad down, but in those days therapy was pretty much for advanced cases and Betty Jean Klipstein. No one even suggested it. As a kind of self-therapy, I took the last few of Dad's Corona Coronas and went around town handing them out to his auto mechanic, his barber, the Klurfeld's down at Auto Parts and Service, anybody I could think of who had known Dad, to let them know he wouldn't be coming by anymore. Clayton was helpful, reassuring me that there was nothing I could have done, which helped, and, later, suggesting that I should consider going away to college, rather than staying at home with Mother, who would be all right. Mom actually flourished in those single years, having to use skills she had not used in thirty-five years of marriage, and, after a year at the university in Milwaukee, I went to Madison just in time for the Dow demonstration and riots, a much needed distraction.

40

Foundling, at Fifty

My dad died when I was a kid, which was bad, but it was quick. Mom lived to be eighty-eight (ninety if you took my brother Howard's accounting for Social Security purposes), which was good, but she was in decline for the last ten or fifteen, which was bad. You can't win. The truisms—"you've got to take the good with the bad," "life has its ups and downs," "you don't know how to dress for this weather"—had long lapsed, although "you don't know whether to laugh or cry" still had currency. Missed were the insights, usually gained on shopping forays downtown: "Michael, there are men who wear rouge," or (at Boston Store) "a colored man held the door for me!" Gone, too, the feisty Goldie who bristled when someone served another customer ahead of her when she had been there first, asked if she was getting off at St. Catherine's, or put the bread on the bottom of the bag, even if it was the new girl. After she had slipped to the point where Arthur had to fly in and kidnap her to San Jose, where he and Clayton could look after her, she was well on her way down the slippery slope, like the alley in winter when she made her way to Barger's bakery for baked ham and onion rolls. While she was at the residential-care euphemism in Santa Clara, I went in to see her once and found her sitting in a wheelchair in the day room. She thought I was a nice-looking young man. "Where's my mother?" she asked me. "Mom, was she just here?" She nodded. "I'm sure she'll be back soon."

I hadn't really gotten what was happening with Mom until, several years earlier, while she was once again living down the hall from her sister Rose in Milwaukee, I had reached for the tea kettle in her kitchen and seen that it was covered in a layer of grease and dust. "I don't cook that much for myself, anymore," Mom said. Geraldine Kahn Feldman, the queen of clean: down on hands and knees scrubbing the linoleum, washing wallpaper (which I've never seen anybody else do), and even boiling utensils during bacteria season, had come to this. It was no coincidence that she had given birth to doctors; you could have operated on our kitchen table. I grew up believing that the ammonia atmosphere of Neptune was nothing unusual, since it pervaded our house. Mom not only did windows; she did them from the outside, as well. Except for seeing Dad on the third and last extension of a rickety ladder painting the house (thank God he never fell on me while I was vainly trying to stop the ladder from shaking—I had trauma enough as a kid), there was nothing that could take my breath away like finding Mom on the top step of a step ladder in the irises shpritzing the kitchen widows with Windex for an unobstructed view of the alley. She washed my trains one time, and the engine stopped working. I never saw a pile of dirty clothes until I went away to college, and those I bagged up and brought home on the Badger bus, figuring she'd know what to do with them. Did I mention she was clean?

Now the handwriting was on the pots. Her sister Rose, who was five years older, had been keeping her afloat; I arranged for a visiting nurse to come in, and then another, as Mom kept throwing them out. She didn't like interlopers. "She wanted me to bend," Mom said of one home invader. Whereas, historically, you always had to tell my mother something twice or three times before she copied, now the number was infinite, and it never did sink in. "Did you call the police to tell them where you're parked?" "Yes, Mom, I called them right when I got here." "Michael, call the police to tell them you're parked on the street." "I did, Mom. I told you." "Make sure you call the police, or they'll give you a ticket." "Right, Mom." If it were up to her, you'd call the police again as soon as you hung up to tell them where you were parked, which is bound to get you a visit from a squad car in Shorewood. About this time, we went out for Mother's Day to Pandel's, a nice restaurant for the Jewish crowd, with a woman I was then seeing. We had to wait, and Mom couldn't stand, so I begged a unused chair from a table for her so that she could gather her wits beneath the coat rack. Afterward, when I asked Mom what she thought of the girl, she said, "She ordered the most expensive thing on the menu," showing she hadn't lost all of her acumen. ("Some of them will take you to the cleaners," Mom's assessment of women, was particularly canny in that she had worked in the family's dry cleaning shop as a girl and had seen it happen more than once.)

I love my family, but Mother was the only one I could talk to when things got rough, because she knew rough. As the youngest daughter, she had gotten the lioness's share of the duties at home; she went to work instead of seventh grade. Dave Feldman must have seemed like her ticket to ride, although, as it turned out, between his health and his trust in the wrong people, that was no picnic, either. Mom was the only one in the family, other than me, who had suffered setbacks. Still, she really didn't have any sage advice when I got married (to a *shiksa*) at twenty-one, lived like a hippie selling beads at craft shows, got divorced, taught school, quit teaching, drove a cab, went broke, got a radio show, quit a radio show, brought all the wrong women around, and got down in the dumps repeatedly, but she always listened and said, "Are you eating?" sending me home with a roast chicken, or a nice brisket, fruit, several pairs of white socks, toll house cookies, maybe a kuegel or a jar of spinach borscht, and, sure enough, that seemed to do the trick. Of course, the checks in the mail—$25, $50—even when, after finally starting to do things right, I didn't need it, were much appreciated. I saved the notes she used to wrap her little somethings in (so you couldn't tell it was a check in the envelope): "Michael, use some of this for warm clothes"; "Michael: Beware of pick pockets"; or, this one on the back of a gift certificate from One-Hour Martinizing, "Michael: Soon your birthday will be here. Better early than late. Talk to you soon. No card (excuse), Love, Mom." Another, on the back of an Ace Hardware coupon, was the classic: "Dear Michael: Please don't think you called for anything else. After all, I'm glad you think of me. Love, Mom." Once, after we had had a spat because I wasn't wearing pants clean enough to go to lunch with her and her ninety-year-old paramour, Al Schneiderman (a fastidious dresser, having been in men's wear for many years), she wrote "Michael: Please call *collect always* as I want to talk to you a lot. *Please.* I will call you soon to come here as I want to talk. P.S. Watch your purse when you cash it." She didn't sign this one, but there was no doubt who it was from, and no doubt how much I continue to miss her, and not for the money.

41

A Feldman Is

(from the *Feldman Handbook*)

A Feldman is always thinking about something else.

A Feldman gets this little smile when he finds himself amusing.

A Feldman comes in law or medicine.

"The Feldman look" is not a fashion statement but, in fact, just the look a Feldman gives.

A Feldman is a cockeyed optimist, flying in the face of his innate sense of futility.

A Feldman believes in the pleasure principle in principle.

A Feldman secretly hopes for reckless abandon.

A Feldman relaxes only under sedation.

Like a gunslinger, a Feldman never sits with his back to the door.

When a Feldman enters a room, heads turn for other reasons.

A Feldman practices preemptive self-deprecation.

A Feldman has never been a matinee idol, although Uncle Ed looked pretty good in his sailor suit.

A bipolar Feldman does not experience the highs.

A Feldman may be broadened, but it is not from travel.

The overweight Feldman is really just four inches shorter than he should be.

A Feldman with good eyes is still in the testing stage.

A Feldman thinks of himself as "in" but not "of."

A Feldman does not brag, and it kills him.

God bless the Feldman that's got his own, because he didn't get any from the previous Feldman.

A Feldman is not rich but may be affluent.

A Feldman's traits are passed on through the father and in spite of the mother.

A Feldman, like a Freud, wonders what it is a woman wants and why she can't leave him alone, already.

A Feldman can be charming if you like that sort of thing.

A Feldman can be outgoing if you know what to look for.

A Feldman is comfortable in front of a crowd but not in front of individuals.

While not religious, a Feldman feels something (tap, tap) here.

A Feldman worships at his own altar.

A Feldman is just Jewish enough to marry in the faith.

A woman married to a Feldman soon realizes it.

Howard aside, a Feldman can do simple mechanical things.

If a Feldman was ever flamboyant, it was not reported.

When a Feldman finds a shirt or a pair of pants he likes, he keeps buying them until they stop making them, and then he tries to special order.

A Feldman likes to have the last word. Conversation between Feldmans is like table tennis between Chinese.

A Feldman believes that a profession is something to fall back on.

A Feldman believes that talking to himself is communicating.

Beneath his soft shell, a Feldman has a soft underbelly.

A Feldman, while often generous, immediately regrets it.

A Feldman should avoid spandex, dairy foods, investments, partnerships, chick films, serious occasions, formal meetings, dance floors, emceeing, black tie, cowboy boots, pouring his own concrete, hanging doors, putting on additions, small-engine repair, going to the mall on Sundays, and chit chat.

A Feldman has "Milwaukee" written all over him. Previously, a Feldman had Kiev written all over him.

Every Feldman thinks he's funnier than every other Feldman, although outsiders would be hard pressed to notice much difference.

A Feldman can flood with nostalgia and sentiment; if this happens, hold his pedal to the floor (do not pump).

42

This Far Apart

As Dad used to say with forefinger an inch from thumb, "Remember, they're only this far apart." Why he would say that to a kid who had no idea what he was talking about until relatively recently, if at all, I don't know. Leaving a legacy may have been the answer. When you think of all the insights you might impart to a child in the short time in which you may impart them, Dad's golden measure was a head scratcher. Over the years, I tried applying it to myriad things before, quite by accident, finding it to be true just at the moment when "that's what he meant!" was a pretty inappropriate thing to blurt out. One would like to think it has a deeper meaning, but one is reluctant to search for it; it could be figurative, like life being a game of inches, or he could have been talking about the thin line that separates dualities such as good/evil, success/failure, or accounts receivable/payable. Pretty clearly, though, knowing Dad, it refers to mistakes of the heart made under the cover of darkness when there is a very small margin for error.

It hasn't been easy to weave a rich fabric of human interactions on the basis of that one thread, what with the warp and the woof being only this far apart. I've had to embellish, and to extrapolate what was not only in the heart but in the mind of the founding father. Examining the phrase talmudically, I've added my commentary to the margins, but it's only this far from the text. My brother Howard, who also received the message (I keep meaning to ask Clayton and Arthur if they did—it's probably like Dad telling each of us individually that we were his favorite, only to find out forty years later that the edifices of our self-esteem were all built on one foundation) and I have compared notes on the solution of the *koan,* and use the gesture as a kind of sign language for hello, goodbye, and peace. Howard thinks Dad may have been playing devil's advocate, but in the end we had to agree it sounded very much like Dave Feldman. Had we been a more ribald family, we might've considered putting it on his stone, what with him and Mother being only this far apart.

Understandably, when I finally did crack the code, I was shocked retroactively for the tousle-haired eleven-year-old it was entrusted to, but it's come in quite handy since; I can hardly measure a door for a frame, reconcile accounts, or look into my spouse's eyes without thinking, "They're only this far apart." This was the gift of a worldly man who, admittedly, didn't have to travel that far between insights, but not a suitable inheritance for a girl child without throwing the door open even wider for feminist revisionist psychotherapists of the near future. I would guess, however, that her mother might have a pearl or two of wisdom not that far afield, possibly also involving thumb and forefinger, that she might share. I only hope that the girls will examine their findings critically, as I have mine, all these years.

43

Anglos in America

Like Dad used to say, only without the italics, "It *tuchise* a long time *putz* we made it, just the same." In an age when a Lieberman can be a serious presidential candidate (finally a Jew, and it's the wrong one), when even clandestine brothers and sisters like John Kerry and Madeline Albright and Wesley Clark can weather the predicted storm of their revelations, when restrictive deeds have given way to a simple wink and a nod, and when we can join any club that would have us for members, we Jews have pretty much made it in the door of the American dream house and might even find an attractive Episcopalian waiting there, should she happen to get home first. Life is good.

I've even had to explain anti-Semitism to my daughters ("Dude," said Ellie, "that frickin' sucks"), who haven't had the advantage of wading into neighborhood religious wars flying the Feldman flag, emblazoned with the star of David A. In postwar Milwaukee (where there had been a lot of sentiment for going in on the German side), the Lutherans hated the Catholics, and the Catholics

196

hated the Lutherans; the only thing they all agreed on were the Jews. Frankly, it wasn't hard to feel like the accursed. As a kid, I always had an alibi ready for where I was in 33 A.D., just in case someone leaped out from the doorway of Mt. Calvary (I thought the name meant they were going to ride in on horses, like the Cossacks), which I had to pass en route to Sherman School, and I was forced to account for my whereabouts. Sometimes it got physical, and those German Lutheran kids ran pretty big. I don't know what they were telling them in there about us, but from the look in their eyes I don't think it was favorable—maybe we were named on the list Martin Luther nailed up. One time a Calvary kid cornered me in the alley behind my Aunt Ida's house (I don't remember the reason, blood lust, maybe) and got me in a pretty good headlock; Aunt Ida, watching in horror from her kitchen window, called my mother, screaming, "They're killing Michael! They're killing Michael!"

Naturally, my buddies were all Lutherans of one synod or another (there was only one other Jewish family on the other side of the block, but they didn't go to Twerski's), but even Roger Ladwig, my best friend, could pull out the surefire "dirty Jew!" conversation stopper when it suited him. I was always a pretty quick kid, but it was a tough straight line to work with. "Dirty Lutheran!" just didn't have the same effect. "Missouri Slimebod!" I didn't think of at the time. You cold hurl "Kraut" at one faction and "Cat-licker" at the other (actually Roger introduced me to the Cat-licker option, but I wasn't comfortable with it), but usually you just tried not to cry and give them the satisfaction. Hard for a kid, though, when what you are is an epithet.

"They're just jealous," Mom used to say, although she never did say of what. She, of course, was prepared to mix it up should anyone even look at her cross-eyed, even those who were unfortunate enough to be cross-eyed. She had her hands full protecting the brood. My era was enlightened compared to that of my older brothers; Clay once started a fire in our next-door neighbors' garage after one of their kids winged a can at Howie's head, drawing certainly not the first blood or the last blood to flow from a theological dispute. They were fighting the War at Home, the Second World, while we were merely irregulars in the uneasy peace that followed.

Eventually, Balkanization occurred in Milwaukee, and every ethnic group and race moved to its respective semiautonomous suburb—Fox Point, Bayside, Grafton, what have you, where you can find them today with nearly identical yards, patios, and gas grills. If the trend toward re-urbanization continues, though, I don't know—hostilities could flare up, but I'm hoping we're past it.

VI

I Was Just Thinking

44

Paranoid's Paradise

These are heady days for the paranoid: vindicated after all these years! The paranoid no longer is: paranoia has outlived its usefulness when everybody is out to get us. The downside is it's getting harder and harder to find an irrational fear to cling to. FDR said there was nothing to fear but fear itself, but that's always been more than enough for me. I can take it from there, no problem. Besides, what's scarier than fear itself? Those who insist on braving it out by saying "You can't live in fear" have never lived my life; you *can,* and I *do.* Meek Feldman, that's me. One day I expect to inherit the earth (and I'm converting it to cash, immediately).

My earliest snapshot shows me, two-ish in a sailor suit of no known navy, on the front lawn of our house in Milwaukee, squinting into the sun and Dad with a look of dread, and I mean *of being.* Trust me, I've seen it in mirror image many times since. My first word was no; I'm told I didn't bother learning another for quite some time. I would cry at the drop of a hat, which, after all, can be frightening for the child imagining a head in it. I still need a lot of reassuring, although anyone who could reassure me is long gone after eventually needing a lot themselves. I reassure little ones these days, but I hope they never ask me if I mean it. I don't. I'm lying through my teeth. Nora, my eight-year-old (and a natural believer), forced me to say I believed in God (she walked around me in circles until I broke), but she could never get me to say that it made me feel any better. Call me Old Testament, but it is a fact that some of the earliest editions appear to have been etched on parchment not unlike human skin, and with a curious dark purple ink. No foil-embossed cut-away covers for our Deity.

My sense of humor, if that's what it is, is such an obvious defense mechanism that I'm embarrassed take any credit for it and certainly no blame. When they keep coming at you, you've got to parry with something. You don't always have a machine gun nest when you need one. Wit is all well and good, but it pales, as do I, in the face of brute strength; in any pen/sword contest, give me whatever's longer and sharper and I'll sign autographs afterward. The fact is, many if not every single one of those poised to harm or kill you in some way would not appreciate a joke at just that moment; in fact, the person probably achieved that head of steam after one of your little harmless *bon mots*. Whatever latitude beauty may have in the eye of the beholder, funny is not readily apparent to all, and, who knows, they may be right. More important, they may be bigger.

Below and beneath that, I'm just not a brave person. Fearless doesn't come to mind when I think of me. I mind dying. I can't put a good spin on it. Maybe I'm not the altruist I should be, but you'd have to push me on top of a grenade because it would be entirely out of character for me to jump on one. Even if it were a dud, I'd be bruised for weeks. (I apologize in advance; if you need a ride somewhere, no problem.) You'll see me running into a burning building only if the fire is hotter outside, and while I'd like to think I'd jump into the Kin-nickinnic to pull someone out, would two bodies washing up in downtown Milwaukee be any better than one (particularly during the holiday rush)? No one really knows what he'll do when the chips are down (a good reason for keeping your chips up), but I doubt the initial adrenalin rush would preclude the permanent and severe back problems you'd have once you lifted the Cutlass off your father, whom, after all, you'd begged to get rid of that car for years.

It would have to be one good day for me to be a hero. Bravery, like red hair, is something you're born with. I don't have red hair. I don't have a brave face. My brave face trembles around the eyes and mouth, or wants to. When I whistle a happy tune, it's the zither theme from *The Third Man* gone frantic as Orson Welles gets shot and falls back down the manhole into the sewers of Vienna (nice sewers, though: roomy). If that isn't life, I don't know what is. Kafka was my bedtime reading during adolescence, and I knew if I were ever transformed into a dung beetle my mother would try to sweep me up in a dustpan and my brother would throw in a rotten apple, which would lodge in my thorax. Kafka must have lived on 58th Street at one time.

About the one thing I'm not afraid of is speaking in public, which just happens to be the number one fear in America, followed closely by going to the dentist. I could speak to a room full of dentists and it wouldn't bother me, although I'm sure it would be like pulling teeth (well, it would be nice to hear *them* groan for a change). The appeal is that when you're in front of a group of people they're not behind you, unless you're working in the round. You have the advantage of being able to see it coming. At all other times around and especially in the center of crowds (particularly when they have formed a ring around you), assume the worst and you won't be far wrong. For me, groups start at about the number five; any less than that and you could be culled into a one-on-one, which is where nearly everything horrible, from marriage to evisceration, occurs, if there's any distance to be traveled there.

Thanks to the times in which I find myself, I even seem to be losing ground. I didn't used to be afraid of flying, or, if I was, it was for all the right reasons, like the plane was likely to fall from the sky from natural causes and not be plunged into one of the national monuments the pilot has jerked me out of a shallow, troubled nap to tell me is visible from the other side of the craft. Frankly, I don't want to see the Washington Monument that badly. Me, the guy who never hears his flight number without inserting "ill-fated" before it, now girding my loins (and it's hard to gird in coach) to tackle anybody who tries to use the lavatory or looks suspicious (when everybody does). Shouldn't this be the job of those seated in the exit rows? If they're unwilling or unable to perform the duties, let them be re-seated. What about first-class noblesse oblige? With the perks come responsibilities. A perp starts toward the cabin; when the guys give the signal to jump up and wrestle him down ("let's roll!"), do I produce a note from Dr. Parks describing my poor herniated L5 and L4 and the resultant sciatica, which prevents me from sitting on the legs of a foreign national? Probably a bad time to look for sympathy. Sure, they can have my belt to secure him, but I'll need it back before Minneapolis, as I won't have a hand to hold up my pants while wheeling through the gold concourse, definitely a security breach in this day and age.

Until now, a fear of powders is one, surprisingly, I'd overlooked, although I never cared for talc. Or maybe it was the barber I didn't like. My mother was a Lysol fanatic, so aerosols or wicks never did sit right with me (for me, air freshener in the toilet is merely icing on a very bad cake). If my mother had become president, we would now be protected by a space-based Lysol interceptor (ironing the mail is something she probably should have been doing for Davy anyway). Household products were assumed to be only inadvertently bad for you, like the x-ray shoe machines that shot roentgen rays up your little short pants; most of them purported to kill germs rather than get them airborne efficiently, although they might have had that effect. I lived in Kenosha for a while near the American Motors plant and did wonder what the paint ethers were doing to us, but at least they weren't doing it at the behest of a foreign power until Chrysler took over. The Milwaukee of my youth had the heady Red Star yeast aroma you drove through on the downtown expressway, the plant being right next to Milwaukee Casket—call us naïve, but the thought of combining the two was unthinkable. Crop dusters, however, have been scary ever since one nearly got Cary Grant, even though spelunking down Jefferson's huge nostril to save Eva Marie Saint was truly terrifying if ultimately worth it.

I'm nostalgic for the days when a disease was just something you got, not something given you; inoculated *against* as opposed to *with* is a distinction you didn't used to have to make. I don't even know which is covered anymore. It's like *Fahrenheit 451,* only with doctors causing disease instead of firemen starting fires. And then the threat of smallpox just when Mom isn't around to ask if I had my shots. (I'm little worried about polio, too. I know I got something in my little behind; I'm hoping it was the booster.) We should know better; we have history enough as an advanced species to know that by stamping out smallpox, we were just asking for it. You can't stamp out anything without it being used against you. Disco came back, and earth shoes. Still, you can't live that way: we must continue to make inroads against disease, and if they're weaponized, they're weaponized. In fact, now that we have the word "weaponized," anything can be, and there is no longer any such thing as a harmless object, which deep in my heart I always knew.

45

A Little Hitler

I was talking to the Rotary in Milwaukee one time (as we say in Milwaukee), and there was a guy in the audience named Hitler. If there's a guy in the audience named Hitler, it pretty much defines a tough crowd, at least for me. But, it went all right, and Hitler seemed to enjoy it as much as anybody.

Afterward, I got a chance to schmooze with Hitler (for the life of me, I can't remember his first name—Al Hitler? Larry Hitler?) and got around (all right, immediately) to asking him why he hadn't changed his name. He said it was his family name and he was proud of it. Came from a long line of Hitlers. He was a Hitler like his father before him and *his* father before him. His children were little Hitlers, his wife a Hitler by marriage, although for some reason she kept her maiden name (Stalin). They get junk mail addressed to "The Hitlers or Current Residents." There's an aluminum "H" on their combination door. If you see a little sign in the park that reads "Hitler Family Reunion," it's them.

He claimed (not that I was pressing him on the issue; made no difference to me) that he was not related to *the* Hitler, that there were a lot of Hitlers at one time and that *he* was really a Shicklegruber anyway, and, quite possibly, he said, Jewish. I let that one pass, but did Hitler-bait him just a bit ("He did restore pride to the German people, wouldn't you say?"), but Hitler wasn't biting, being long practiced, I would guess, in letting this sort of thing slide. "I really enjoyed your presentation" was pretty much all he would volunteer. I was a hit with Hitler. In *The New Yorker* or somewhere there had just recently been a piece about *the* extended Hitler family, but I didn't recall seeing any Als or Larrys in Milwaukee, which, you'd think, would've been worth a mention. Milwaukee, where the Bund used to have the best dances and where the German Feldmans clipped their final "n" after that first little wave of resentment caused by the Kaiser, would have felt like home to the Hitler *mishpocha*.

But no, he was just a nice guy named Hitler who belonged to the Rotary and who gets kidded about it all the time and responds, I must say, with humor. Still, I think "Hodges" would serve him well, or "Hill," although that's a little close, you know, to "Heil."

46

Barney Google

On a whim, I Googled Barney Google: 67,800 results in .30 seconds, including the lyrics to the Billy Rose and Con Conrad 1923 song:

> Barney Google, with the goo-goo-goo-ga-ly eyes.
> Barney Google bet his horse would win the prize.
> When the horses ran that day, Spark Plug ran the other way.
> Barney Google, with the goo-goo-goo-ga-ly eyes.
>
> Barney Google, with the goo-goo-goo-ga-ly eyes.
> Barney Google had a wife three times his size
> She stood Barney for divorce
> Now he's living with his horse
> Barney Google, with the goo-goo-goo-ga-ly eyes.

Sixty-seven thousand seven hundred and ninety-nine other hits, but none of this stature. I know because I Googled Google, getting 32,100,000 results in a mere .25 seconds, although a goodly number of them were anti-Google, like Google Watch:

Google Watch

Google Watch. A look at how **Google**'s monopoly, algorithms, and privacy policies are undermining the Web. **Google** cookies. Why we target **Google**. Is **Google** God? ...
Description: Argues that **Google**'s privacy policies are undermining the Web.
Category: Computers > Internet > Searching > Search Engines > Google
www.google-watch.org/—Similar pages

Algorithms are not Al Gore's collection of dance music but, apparently what makes search engines like Google possible; unfortunately, I didn't get them in high school (when I was as smart as I ever got), and I don't get them now. Especially the algorithmic notion of the

traveling salesman

(classic problem)
Definition: Find a *path* through a *weighted graph* which starts and
    ends at the same *vertex,* includes every other vertex exactly once,
    and minimizes the total cost of *edges.*
Also known as TSP.
See also *bottleneck traveling salesman, Hamiltonian cycle, optimiza-*
    tion problem, Christofides algorithm, similar problems: *all pairs*
    shortest path, minimum spanning tree, vehicle routing problem.
Note: Less formally, find a path for a salesman to visit every listed
    city at the lowest total cost.
The above described path is always a *Hamiltonian cycle,* or tour;
    however, a Hamiltonian cycle need not be optimal. If the tri-
    angle inequality does not hold, that is $d_{ik} > d_{ij} + d_{jk}$ for some $i, j,$
    k, there is no possible polynomial time algorithm which guaran-
    tees near-optimal result (unless $P = NP$).

Seems harmless enough, just the old Hamiltonian tour of vertexes, yet for some Google is the anti-Christ prophesied by Forbes, the

Capitalist Tool, in 1995 in a cover story on meta-Web searches taking over the world. Thomas Friedman even asked, in the *New York Times,* "Is Google God?" (wouldn't that be Godle?); after a cursory search of the 63,800,000 names of God divined quicker than a lightning bolt, the answer would seem to be "dunno." The Assemblies of God, with which I feel some affiliation, having driven by the campus in Springfield, Missouri, says, on its official Web site, "God is our refuge and strength," both terms of which can be searched on Google and your own conclusions drawn. If faith is the pursuit of faith, a third of a second of your time will get you right into the fray. Faith is undoubtedly being pursued in many of the 200 million searches going on right now, although an ungodly number are undoubtedly looking for a closer walk with "Asian Love Babes."

While that gets me thinking about the mysteries of the Orient (which I once or twice Googled by Occident), I resist, since they tend to leave cookies on your hard drive while the screens just cascade. The things we do for Asian love! Better to refine my search, so on to "google, the number" (frankly, confusing it with googol, which a land-based dictionary revealed to be 10 to the 100th power), and in .32 of a second I had 2,410,000 misconceptions, one of them serendipitously providing this intriguing tidbit:

Goshen Woods: **Google** + Phone **Number**

. . . **Google** + Phone **Number.** I found out today that if you go to **Google** and put your name in the search box you will get your

Name
Address
Phone Number
Links to Yahoo Maps and Map Quest for "conveniently"
    locating your house

I did and conveniently located Child and Youth Services for my area code, in Dane and Dodge Counties, Wisconsin. Andy, seemingly hidden somewhere in the Goshen Woods of the Virginia countryside, however, found himself and did not like it:

> I don't know about the anyone else, but I have a *big* problem with any Joe Schmoe being able to find our house by simply typing our phone number in the google search box. Thankfully, you can remove your info from google by clicking on the phone book icon, reading the instructions and putting the appropriate information in a form.

Posted by Andy at July 2, 2003, 10:16 A.M.

Naturally, I was curious who this Joe Schmoe was harassing Andy, and in a .09 second blink of an eye discovered (among the 17,900 entries) that:

He is running for President.

He fronts "San Francisco's most efficient band" with two ukuleles and a '70s-era analog synth.

He may, according to a physician responding to a Joe Shmoe query, want to take a look at venlafaxine, a dual-action antidepressant that works faster than a single-action AD like fluoxetine or nefazodone.

Venlafaxine, as I now realize after skimming 71,600 results quicker (.17 seconds) than it could kick in,

> is a structurally novel antidepressant for oral administration. It is chemically unrelated . . . to tricyclic, tetracyclic or other available antidepressant agents. Modest increases in blood pressure are to be expected; those with renal diseases should adjust their dosage.

Since this was getting a little depressing, I decided to Google myself, just for the self-stim (what the heck) and found, among the 361,000 of us (although many are redundant), that, besides the

Michael Feldman who told Al Gore, on the way to his concession speech, to can it and turn around, that I was mixed up with Dr. Michael B. Feldman, Professor of Computer Science (so hitching his wagon to my star is no accident) at George Washington University; Michael Feldman, who claims to be at Harvard Law but posted a bouquet toss of dubious academic value on his blog; and the mechanical engineer Michael Feldman of the Technion-Israel Institute of Technology in Haifa, Israel, whose main interests seem to be vibration engineering and signal processing. He emigrated in 1991 from Kurgan, Russia, not far from where we suspect our people come from, but a look at his family tree, the Volls, did not ring any bells.

Then it turns out there's a Michael Feldman who is a writer on *Boston Common,* as well as the unusually annoying *That's So Raven!* (which Nora just loves) on the Disney Channel, starring the grown-up and overchild star of the *Cosby Show* as a clairvoyant whose eyes bulge out whenever she has a vision, and she has a lot of them. Now when I criticize the show to Nora, I have only myself to blame. Ironically, my *Whad'ya Know?* CD is being offered, for $6.99 (cheap), under his credits on the Tome celebrity Web site where I, Michael Feldman, might as well be chopped liver. This took me back to venlafaxine, and whether it was worth looking at the counterindications again; I was goo-goo-goo-ga-ly'd out.

47

Letters from the Milky Way

September 3: Sounding more like an antebellum bodice ripper than a fundamental force of nature, dark energy is the still to be confirmed antigravity predicted by Danny Dunn that pushes the envelope filled with everything there is in the cosmos from the inside out, faster and faster. This should be a good thing, all in all, since, thanks to entropy, if your universe is not expanding, it's contracting, and we'll end up with something about the size of the grapefruit we started with (something there is in nature loves the size of a grapefruit), possibly setting the stage for an even bigger bang should God choose to juice it one more time. But for now it is making space emptier and emptier, and I can't help but take it personally. Some cosmologists, who despite popular belief do not apply makeup to dead people, believe there is a series of universes like sluice ponds, one slopping over into another, with life existing in spots where, by chance, it can, if only, like fishing, you know where to look. This is supposed to make us feel better?

September 7: Sorry I didn't write for the past few days, but I was bummed out. It's silly, since most of this won't play out for billions of years, long after my matter has been converted into a disappointing amount of energy, even seen through a gravitational lens. Still thinking about dark energy—Quintessence, which sounds like a lemon-lime drink and not the vacuum that is sucking us (or maybe more of a leaf blower blowing us) into infinity. At night I find myself holding onto the bedpost. I wish I had never read the *Science Times*—every Tuesday there's more to worry about. This dark energy (not to be confused with dark matter, merely the 99 percent of existence we can't find—even though we're in it—because it doesn't glow) is the three-quarters of the universe by weight (allowing for some settling) that must exist like ghost riders in the sky, keeping it all heading up, moving out (Rawhide!) at stampede velocity as the red shift of the most distant stars suggests. The prior consensus, which we all felt pretty good about, had been that the universe, while still expanding, was slowing down somewhat, only to be expected according to our own humble anecdotal observations of life on earth. Not everyone agrees that dark energy is the cause: you can still tweak gravity and have it come out the same, if you've a mind to, but that's considered cheating, and a can of worms that even Einstein closed after he opened, calling it the greatest mistake he'd ever made, which, mind you, includes not getting it on with Marilyn Monroe when she reportedly was into it. Einstein retracted his "cosmological constant," a repulsive force that kicks in once things get way out of hand, even though it would provide much needed balance for a universe tumbling over the edge of the cosmic stream.

September 9: Took a day with the kids at a water park in the Dells. Rushing down long, wet black tubes only made me think I was dark energy heading toward oblivion. When I got back, I read that from Pittsburgh, even, they can see a hot spot in the cosmic microwave background that shouldn't be there, which, you guessed it, can (only?) be explained by dark energy making a repulsive gravitational well, causing light that passes through it to exit with more energy than it entered with, only true here on earth at Noah's Ark (water park). They said they'd need an accelerator larger than a small galaxy to confirm these results, but not in this economy they don't. One guy said we need a new Einstein to figure it all out, and while we're at it how about a new Gandhi, a new Lincoln, and a new Ernie Kovacs? If they don't occur naturally, we should set about trying to make 'em—they saved Einstein's brain, didn't they? Actually, he's lucky he's dead, because these string theorists, who refuse to wind it up and go away, would kill him. All right, instead of a point, a string, I'll bite, but ten dimensions instead of three, the last seven curled up like loops in a carpet? I don't care what this describes, I want no part of it. It doesn't even make sense as broadloom. At first, string theory couldn't account for dark energy, potentially a relief, but now they managed to weave the strings of numbers into a cosmic relief map you might see at a science fair, made out of salt in a full Todd-A-O ten dimensions with every point—string—on the grid operating under its own fundamental principles and oblivious to its neighbors. Some elegant solution. This is what you get when you ask only one thing of people, a grand unifying theory. And don't start me on strange quarks.

September 16: I don't think it's scientific to use the word "abyss," and I wish they'd stop doing it. That's more from *Pilgrim's Progress*, like the Slough of Despond, which, apparently, we should consider ourselves lucky to be in. Maybe the universe wasn't designed for us, or we for it, but we have to carry on as if it were, or we were, don't we? Negative emotions weaken your response to the flu vaccine (NYT Health and Fitness, 9/3/03); imagine the havoc wreaked by perceiving existence to be a tangle of rubber bands stretched to snapping, or ten-dimensional bubbles blowing bubbles blowing bubbles, all at the speed of light to create and deflate universes. Try wrapping your mind around that. It's bad enough one universe can rupture and another form like a polyp; we should have universes passing other universes like kidney stones? This is too close to home and makes me so uncomfortable to think about that I have to sign off now, even though I had a lot more I was thinking about.

September 19: "The decay of the cosmological constant will be fatal, experts agree." The one thing they agree on. Forget for a moment we'll never begin to understand what it is they're even arguing about; it'll be over before we even know what hit us. I can't even get excited about the asteroid hurtling toward the earth. It would be a kindness, really, rather than having to watch the carpet unravel from inside the nap. Forget dark energy, dark matter—I can see why dark ages occur. The Pope was right to stop Galileo, just another guy who thought the world revolved around him. It's a blessing the guy at the Space Telescope Institute hasn't found the supernova he needs of just the right age to confirm our worst fears of a sea of dark energy roiling between it and us, making our increasing emptiness all but inescapable. Revoke his Hubble privileges. Let the telescope re-enter and burn up. Don't send up another. Find out how much of this is tax supported. Look into the grants, not the stars. Cancel the *Times*. While there is still time.

48

Baby Boomers Go Boom!

The bloom is off the Baby Boomers; we are now the Over-the-Counter culture. This is the dawning of the Age of Thin-Hairius. The world was right to dread this millennium, not for any apocalyptic or kabbalistic reasons but for the fact that it marks the time when the Boomers will begin to go boom and no one will be safe from the shrapnel. Already we're beginning to pop like corn. Since I'm handy, let me use myself as an example. I'm in what Dad used to call good shape for the shape I'm in; I'm no Greek maxim, but I don't do anything much to excess, especially exercise (you can argue, but my lower back was in mint condition until just last summer when I made the mistake of bussing my daughter's fruit plate off the floor and, instead, joined it), and I am admirably virtuous due to the inconvenient hours required not to be, in these days when an "all-nighter" means not getting up to go to the bathroom. Fourth of four sons (three sons and an ethnic orientation short of a blues song), I was born in 1949 (March 14, if you'd care to jot it down), and therefore saw in the year 2000 at age fifty, auspicious for me, but probably not the fulcrum upon which the third millennium teeters. (On the other hand, this is 5764 in the Jewish calendar and the millennium is really 236 years away, so I still have time to make reservations on the QE II.) With a stiff tail wind I should flutter through several more decades in relatively good health (once I stop getting childhood diseases from my grade schoolers) and can reasonably expect a healthy sex life into my seventies, although, apparently, not before. So what's my problem?

For starters, I'm now in the decade, the fifties, I most clearly associate with my father, which would give me a warm feeling all over had he not died at sixty. Thanks to better nutrition and a move to a climate where they don't shovel snow, my oldest brother, Clayton, is now older than my dad (sort of like the contradiction cosmologists face with the stars being older than the universe), breaking the tape for Feldman longevity. He looks like the man to beat, but you never know. Through bad nutrition and a sedentary lifestyle, my hope is to prove the pundits wrong and earn the opportunity to attribute my impressive age to whatever I damn well please: plum brandy, Cholula sauce, shallow breathing, chicken fat. Meanwhile there are the not-so-subtle inklings of betrayal by the body I've gone out of my way to be nice to over the years (despite its obvious shortcomings): having to watch how I pull open a door, stepping off a curb only on my good foot (the left), bracing myself for a sneeze so my back won't take the brunt, living to see my thighs become a body issue (thank God men don't feel free to discuss such things). When I confided to eight-year-old Nora that I was getting old, she said, "Dad, you *are* old." She is, however, convinced that my bald spot is growing back in, and who am I to disabuse a child?

Most of this probably wouldn't hit home so hard if home weren't a college town filled with reminders of how I'm not like the other kids, particularly when it comes to really long T-shirts and cavernous low-slung cargo pants (and the hip-hoppers wear 'em *backward*) with one's Calvins sticking out intentionally. Thanks to styles having come around again after thirty years, young women today look just like they did in 1968, but what appears to be Ramona is actually the youngest daughter from her second marriage. While I can still dare to eat a peach and win, venturing out I see young people in what appears to be a parallel (or perhaps perpendicular) universe; how they manage to spill beer from another dimension onto my walkers is a mystery. Someone my own age inevitably shows up, crammed into a pair of rivet-popping un-relaxed Levis and a Dead T-shirt (what does he think I'm trying to prove, anyway?), and I flee to a neutral bar rail before he flashes a peace sign and blows my cover. It's pathetic how some people can't accept their age.

Still, I think we put too much emphasis on age; as I get older I think that more and more. I mean, prick me, do I not bleed? What is age, anyway, but general degradation of all body systems and mental capabilities, many of which were not that great to begin with? Historically, we'd be dead by now, something worth bearing in mind, at least as long as you can hold on to the thought. Middle age might be a Victorian invention, after all, like childhood (before then, they were just little annoying people). I could be losing my remaining hair and putting on weight for nothing. Regardless, it's better than it's going to get; you can make hay at dusk, too, what with headlights on the tractor. After all, you can't be a baby forever.

49

What Crisis?

A study on successful midlife development by the MacArthur Foundation Research Network concludes that the "midlife crisis" is a myth. This means that I'm putting on weight and losing hair for nothing. Only 23 percent of the participants in the study—some 3,000 Americans ages twenty-five to seventy-four—reported having a midlife crisis. My guess is that the 23 percent cluster somewhere around the middle of the group surveyed, since very few twenty-five-year-olds would be having a midlife crisis unless they were convinced they would live only to fifty. At the deep end, a seventy-four-year-old having midlife problems is really quite the optimist and not to be concerned about, at least until he hits 120 or so. Those remaining—averaging around age fifty—would be your 23 percent, proving, if nothing else, that it is those in midlife who tend to have midlife crises.

If the study's figures are spot on, 23 percent of any population that suffers a disorder of this magnitude should be considered a pandemic worthy of calling out the National Guard and stockpiling antitoxins—Viagra, Minoxidil, Cutty Sark, Extra Strength Excedrin in non-childproof caps, Freedent—in condo community centers and retirement villages across the snowbird belt, but I don't see it happening, and it won't if the idea that it's an illusion becomes the conventional wisdom. It would be ironic, at the very least, if this band of middle years were the only one without a bona fide associated disorder, but maybe these years are the eye of the storm. Any study that calls itself the Research Network on Successful Midlife Development, though, has a built-in bias: a Research Network on Unsuccessful Midlife Development would find something vastly different, some personal and societal holocaust requiring heroic measures, not denial. Don't forget, this is the MacArthur Foundation, the same people who, year after year, refuse to give me an open-ended genius grant.

Why would a young fella like myself even be concerned about midlife? Well, you're not going to believe this, but I turned fifty a few years ago, and you can imagine how hard that is for a thirty-four-year-old. Half-empty, half-full—what do I care, it's still half. I knew the jig was up when I got an offer in the mail that said, "One week left to buy life insurance," and when I found myself asking for the special at the Olive Garden because I couldn't read the menu without removing the magnifier specs from my wallet and applying them, pince-nez, over my specs in front of the attractive young woman I was having a strictly deductible lunch with. Apparently the MacArthur kids don't have these moments. I raged against the dying of the light by maintaining a low-grade, long-term depression for most of the key year and forbade a fiftieth birthday party featuring the inevitable gag gifts: the Depends adult diapers, the Efferdent gift set, the Viagra bottle filled with little blue jelly beans (or so I discovered the not-so-hard way), the little crutch that guys who can woodwork a little crank out for the humorous support of your "third leg," and the cards like "Let's hear it for Fifty . . . Hip, Hip, Replacement!" I thought I was home free when, on the weekend of my birthday, who (pl.) of all people but my radio audience (or, as I like to think of them, people who come to see a radio show) brought me every one of those gifts, plus the playing cards ("You know you're fifty when . . ."), the book *50: The Age of Wheezin'*, a voodoo doll to stick pins into my aches and pains, and a toothbrush from a dentist emblazoned "Brush 'em while you still got 'em."

Amazingly, it worked. I felt much better, particularly in the Depends. I'm beginning to accept and even play the age card; given a choice in midlife options between an SUV and a woman half my age, I went with the one with the better warranty (three years/36,000 on the power train beats anything I'm likely to find on a like-new twenty-five-year-old). When I first wedged it into the garage, my wife called it an "obscenity"; the name stuck. I'd paint it on the door but for the resale impact. If it turns out anything like my last car (a '93 Accord), it'll see just 30,000 around-town miles in the next seven years and never get out of 2WD. (I'm not even sure how to put it in four—am I on the fly or ain't I?) Still, you never know—just one washed-out mountain road along the Nevado Huascaran in Peru and the drive train pays for itself. If I might be permitted to rationalize my options: moon roof, no defense; heated leather seats, a little too obviously as close or as warm as I will again get to the genuine hide of another; and the trailer hitch—well, you never know when you might run into something you might want to pull. Maybe a big long trailer like Lucy and Desi's, in which my premenopausal spouse can collect souvenir boulders (particularly if, like Desi's Airstream, it detaches on the fly). Today, of course, owning an SUV makes you an accessory to terrorism, but at the time it didn't come with that package. If you want to schlep terrorists, you're better off with a van with the fold-down row of seats. For the few miles I drive, it's a pleasure. The earth, all right, but who else does it hurt? It was either one SUV or two Priuses.

A cry for help this may be, but it's one that won't be heard over the Bose system with the six-CD changer in the dash, stocked with dead artists and defunct bands that keep the interior at a constant 1965, where I can suffer in the Sound of Silence. Why should I be immune now, when I've been sucked into every other maelstrom described by Gail Sheehy in *Passages*—Birth, Toddler, Early Childhood, Childhood, Early, Late, and Way-Late Adolescence, Early Adulthood, Adulthood, Late Junior Chamber of Commerce, and Presenile Crises—and weathered them all, if badly. This, too, shall pass, and with my butt a comfortable four feet off the road in the catbird seat, a vantage point I couldn't have afforded earlier.

 50

Why I've Got a Loverly Bunch of Coconuts

My birth song, the tune that was playing on the Zenith to mask the fact of my conception, was "I've Got a Loverly Bunch of Coconuts," by none other than Merv Griffin doing a bad cockney accent. That would explain a lot, if, as they say, your birth song has a bigger influence on your life than your rising sign. And it doesn't stop there: Nat Cole's 1949 hit "Nature Boy" ("There was a boy / A very strange enchanted boy") greeted me upon my arrival from St. Joseph's, while Kay Kayser's "Woody Woodpecker" filled our half of the duplex while my susceptible little brain was still folding over like the egg whites in Mom's Mixmaster. I played my oldest brother Clayton's 78's (Clay's a talented guy with questionable taste in music) and managed to imprint the entire Frankie Laine catalogue, including the "Gandy Dancer's Ball" (where "they dance on the ceiling, they dance on the wall"; fact is, those gandy dancers'll dance just about anywhere. For the record, the railroads were the "MKT, the old SP, the Lehigh Valley, too; the C&J, the Santa Fe, the Southern and the Soo"), "Moonlight Gambler," in which Frankie gambles for love and loses, and oh what heartaches it causes him, a lesson well learned by "The Rock of Gibraltar," where, while selling brushes door to door, "when it looks for certain, a lady might be flirtin', / I tell her I'll be back in thirty days." It's Frankie (who just turned ninety, I read) I have to thank for my preconception of woman as "Jezebel," which I've had the hardest time shaking.

I cried to Johnny Ray's "Cry" (because "you'll feel better if you cry") and hid along with the little white cloud, who cowered around the older thunderheads. No thanks to Phil Harris, I learned early on that "Some Little Bug Will Get [Me] Some Day" ("So? You wanna live forever?"). Well, he was the "Ding Dong Daddy of Dumas," so I guess he knew what he was doing. To show you the way things were going, Jo Stafford had me believing that some day my shrimp boat would come in, but, until then, "it's a treat to beat your feet on the Mississippi mud" because "Mr. and Mrs. Sippi" make you feel at home. I had faith in Percy Faith, particularly in something, I don't know, delicious happening during "Delicado," and wanted badly to knock three times, whisper low, and be in "Hernando's Hideaway," which may, in fact, have been "number fifty-four, the house with the bamboo door." There was a hot piano playing behind the green door, "don't know what they're doing but they laugh a lot behind the green door." I pictured "Reefer Madness," although I bet Clay didn't.

Clearly, music messes with your mind; they've even found the center in the brain it pickles: be still my aching rostromedial prefrontal cortex. Your mind has a heart of its own, and here's where it is, just behind the third eye, a third ear, where genuine emotion and the musical kind confuse each other. Popular music, indelibly and without need of life experience, wires your emotional response to all future love, loss, and longing, Tin Pan Alley's lock, schlock, and barrel.

It gets you under your skin, night and day, under the hide of you. It does something to you, something that simply mystifies you. All they have to do to is begin your beguine to drop the needle on you and play you like a 78. It still works with digital: among her (currently) 138 shared songs on Kazaa, my daughter Ellie has Eminem singing "My penis is the size of a peanut, have you seen it?" as well as John Mayer's equally disturbing "Your Body Is a Wonderland" and another one about how she's the one the other girl's boyfriend wants. This all, apparently, has meaning for Ellie, and so I must respect it, but, as our parents did, you can't help wondering about long-term effects.

I know songs got to me. I can remember practically howling out my bedroom window in the general direction of Uptown Motors when "I'm So Lonesome I Could Cry" came on, particularly when it happened to coincide with the 9:05 Milwaukee Road freight blowing its horn at the Sherman Boulevard crossing; it wasn't the source Hank Williams drew from, but it worked for me. Somehow I knew, even then, that once a robin cries, things have gotten really bad. Why a ten-year-old would be so lonesome he could cry like a robin can only be answered by a very close reading of the text of "Deep Purple." Three brothers, two parents, and Uncle Max hanging around all the time, and I was so lonesome I could cry. Suffice it to say you can miss someone you've never met except in song; in fact, you miss them more. It was the ballads our parents should have worried about, not "Tutti Frutti." Lenny Welch's "Since I Fell for You"—"You made me leave my happy home" nearly made me leave my happy home, and for nothing. There was no "you"; there still isn't, and it's the "you" that gets you—"*You* Send Me," "when I want *you*, all I have to do is dream" (make that all I do do), "I love *you*, *you-you-you-you-you*." Were Gene McDaniels a "Tower of Strength," he'd "watch *you* cry" (setting aside the fact I thought it was a "Tower of String" for the longest time, and it still made sense). Then or now,

I could never muster the nonchalance of a Tommy Edwards—how did I know what was in the game or even what the game was, or how Conway Twitty knew "It's Only Make Believe" and made me believe it? I still believe it.

51

My Life, The Musical

I write the songs that make the young girls want to listen to something else, at least if they're my daughters. "You wrote that?" scoffs Ellie. At least I think she was scoffing—whatever it is, she does it a lot of it.

"The words. John wrote the music." The song playing was "Even Jesus Don't Love Me:"

> Times are hard
> Not just for me.
> I wonder how bad
> It can be.
> I look to heaven and I see
> Even Jesus
> Don't love me.

"Don't people mind that?" asked Nora.

"No, they don't mind." How could they—they'll never hear it. "It's not meant to offend. It's about a guy who feels so unloved that even Jesus, who loves everybody (they say), doesn't love him."

"That's dissin' Christians," said Ellie, always ready to spring to the defense of a majority.

Well, here I was losing yet another argument with a yet another female about my intentions. "Here, listen to this one," I said, and played a cut that Johnny Cash might have sung, "I'm Not Dead":

> Today they say
> They're going to put me down
> And lay these poor old bones down in the ground.
> But when the service ends and all is said
> Don't drop me yet 'cause
> I'm not dead.

The girls look perplexed, or troubled, or maybe one of each. "It's about a man who's dead but doesn't know it," I explained. "He thinks he's talking to the guys taking him to the cemetery—trying to stop the procession. He's trying to talk them out of burying him, because he thinks he isn't dead, even though he is. It's supposed to be funny." I was dead, and I knew it. I probably shouldn't have opened with those two for these two. Well, I don't get a lot of their songs, either, like "Country Girl," where the hip-hopping homey who falls in love with a country girl (who does Jello shots and gets only broadcast TV) turns out to be a white boy from the 'burbs, albeit heavily tattooed, in real life. For me that ruins the whole concept, unless she happens to be an African American country girl, which I would applaud. "She (Fuckin') Hates Me" I can at least relate to, but it's the exception. If Ellie keeps playing "P.I.M.P.," I just may have to put my foot down.

What my daughters fail to appreciate is that my life is a musical, the lack of action and mumbled narrative interrupted periodically (and, apparently, for no reason) by songs of yearning, despair, and elation (or what I would imagine elation to be) that I've written with my pal John Sieger. Our collaboration started back in Kenosha twenty-five years ago, when we were two points on a triangle, my ex (and his then-present) being the apex. This turned out to be bonding (triangles are quite stable, you know, although buckyballs are really the way to go): I used to go see John's band play, and dance with her to songs I'd written about the former us sung by the present him. (If you think the grammar is problematic, you should have lived the life.) This menage-a-rie may not have been healthy, but it was musically inspiring, although the first song we did had nothing to do with any of this: I was still shoveling shit from my ex-horses (John would soon be the one mucking out her Stygian stables) and living the solitary life in the cement-block cabin of our wooded day camp, when I stepped into something in a country vein:

> If my old man were alive today
> This world would kill him quick.
> For all this so-called progress
> He wouldn't give a lick.
> You wouldn't find him sympathizing
> With people just plain sick.
> If my old man were alive today
> This world would kill him quick.

It went on from there. It really was my neighbor, Jim Delwich, talking; he was forever saying that the way things were done nowadays would have killed his dead father. My old man would certainly be astounded by current accounting practices. John set what I meant to be an amusing verse to a much more evocative tune than it deserved; the unaccustomed taste of sincerity was, for me, intoxicating. That opened the floodgates. Here I was, alone, living in the middle of the woods with leftover animals, feeling emotions that it was thought Feldmans were incapable of (having "the full range of Feldman emotion" was our disclaimer), and with nobody to tell it to except my dog and my composer. The dog turned out some nice stuff, too. I must have written about a hundred lyrics that year, trying to work things out on the back of envelopes, like Lincoln did at Gettysburg, and maybe lure her back. Early on, I must admit, I did write a lyric advising him to ditch her: "Forget her, she'll change your tune if you let her . . ." but some guys can't take a hint. She wouldn't dance to that one. Better, I suppose, was a simple plea I could make, Cyrano-like, through my not-so-small-nosed-either friend:

> Were I born
> A gypsy man
> I'd take you for my prize,
> Steal you in
> My caravan
> And watch the country
> Passing in your eyes.
> Want to love you,
> Want to hold you
> Close to me.

John was having better results, but he was doing the singing. But there's something to be said for wallowing:

> Waited this morning,
> Sun never rose.
> Don't sound like a good sign
> I don't suppose.
> May be a phase
> It's going through.
> Maybe you took it
> With you.

Maybe, and maybe you're clinically depressed, man. Obviously, self-therapy was called for:

> Take heart.
> You ought to feel glad.
> Though the good times don't last,

234

Neither do the bad.
And if you weren't here
Who'd play your part?
All things considered, my friend,
Take heart.

And my late-in-life magical mystery tour when, back in Madison and holed up with a notebook, a glass of wine, and a dog radiating heat like a slag furnace thanks to the pink windowpane I had scored thinking, at age twenty-nine, that it was time to try acid, I intuited that the sea, human blood, and tears (I stopped with bodily fluids there) all had basically the same salinity, and that had to mean something:

Mamma told me
Take it with a grain of salt.
Now I know
Just what she was talking about.
All those lonely years
Crying those salty tears.
I ain't gonna cry
Salty tears no more.

My mother did say that, which is why I carry a grain of salt with me at all times, although I don't always remember to add it. This song actually made it onto John's Warner Brothers record (back when there still were Warner brothers) of the same name, *Salty Tears,* along with several others. As of only a few years ago, it was still selling in Norway, although there's some guy named Michael Feldman who's been living in Florida on my royalties, or at least as far as four hundred bucks can take you in Sarasota.

Phoenix-like, and with the aid of the e-mail undreamed of in our earlier collaboration, all this sprang to life again last year around the holidays, when world events and my usual Christmas depression conspired to put me in the frame of crafting a world solver, you know, one of those songs that tries to make the world right by being much more optimistic about the possibilities of life on earth than the evidence suggests. Plus, Jews write the best Christmas songs, although "Maybe Next Christmas" would not pass for Irving Berlin:

> Maybe next Christmas
> There'll be joy in this world,
> Peace and earth for every
> Boy and girl.
> But if it all ends right now
> No one would miss us
> Maybe next Christmas.

Yes, I know—the uplift takes place in the third verse:

> Our hearts will soar
> Our spirits will lift us
> Maybe next Christmas
> Maybe next Christmas.

52

Fathers and Sons

It was, after all, Philip the Pretty Good, but Alexander the Great: Macedonian culture, like Pharonic Egyptian, motivated sons to eclipse fathers—when you say "Ramses" (in most circumstances) it's II you're talking about, the one with the really big statues, and not his old man. In fairness, Philip II was the man who conceived and assembled the civil and military organizations his son later loosed on the world, having more than one-upped his own sire, Philip I, now relegated to the semilegendary.

Alexander, with the help of Isocrates, the Karl Rove of his day, and Parmenion, the Tommy Franks, picked up where his father left off when assassinated (some say at the behest of the mother, Olympias, anxious to get on with the birthright), leaving the still weak Greek coalition incapable of taking on the tyrant Darius (who outsmarted his own father on a Darius) and the cavalry, chariots, and armada of his estimable Persian Empire. Darius, with paternal pressures of his own (being the III), was Alexander's inherited nemesis. At the Thrilla' in Gaugamela, in present-day Iraq, Alexander routed

Darius's troops in a rematch (the first face-off having taken place at Issus, in Turkey), but Darius once again eluded capture (Alexander never did get him; he died, unexpectedly, of natural causes). While the Persians celebrated early gains by looting and acting for all the known world like an undisciplined horde, peach-cheeked Alexander, fighting at the head of his armies in the days when commander-in-chief meant something, was earning his sobriquet. There was much shock and awe. Darius's much-feared weapons of mass destruction, fifteen long-range elephants, seemed to have had little effect on the outcome other than crushing Alexander's dog, Peritas the Greyhound.

With the Greeks in disarray and the Huns not yet restless, there were no serious challenges to Persian dominance until the precocious Alexander stood up on his hind legs and began begetting Alexandrias (Kandahar was one, Afghanistan being an early conquest), bringing the promise of Athenian democracy (rule by the people, rich and white) to the boonies and ensuring a steady flow of olive oil back the other way. Alexander thought his father (known to raise a chalice) irresolute and criticized him and the old guard for their military shortcomings, even though it was Philip who had revolutionized the phalanx by putting cavalry at the tip and giving the guys in back longer spears, the same light, fast configuration that the son would use to expand the franchise from Africa to Asia Minor. Alexander felt that his father had given up on sieges too early, that he had held back, lacking the taste for annihilation that his son showed right off the bat at smoking, lifeless Thebes.

It's hard to conquer the world, even if it's only the known world, and not get grandiose. Alexander had his handsome (at least that was the official rendition), beardless visage painted, stamped, or chiseled on the appropriate medium wherever he went and even became a god after conquering Egypt, where he needed little convincing that he was not Philip's son, after all, but Ammon Ra's. He started sporting

robes and tiaras for streetwear. The fact is, he never did much of anything with the world other than conquering it, except for the sym-
bolic and yet literal marriage of (old) Europe and Asia, during which
he and a thousand of his closest field commanders (many of whom
were already married, including our hero) took select Asian girls in
troth, Alexander characteristically adding insult to injury by choosing one of Darius's daughters (the thin one). Plutarch got off on
Hellenization, but the fact is the Mongols would eventually make a
much more through job of it, overriding any Hellenic genetic advantage. Other than that, after enjoying the fruits of his labor in
Babylon on the banks of the Euphrates in 323 B.C., Alexander got as
drunk as his father ever had and woke up dead, that being the cue
for all his extended families, fiefdoms, and significant others to mur-
der one another, for the coins to go out of circulation, and for the
known world to kick back on its heels awhile, waiting upon the next
great white, yellow, or black hope, or maybe his son.

53

Making the World Safe for -Ocracy

The general at the Pentagon was absolutely right when, during the looting, he said that the Iraqis were going to have to get serious about the kind of government they want. In their defense, it's a little hard to think "unicameral . . . bicameral?" when you're being shocked and awed; despite a huge effort to get the word out, not everybody knew that Tomahawks were the harbingers of democracy, something we just take for granted. To some extent, those getting out the message were themselves hampered by their lack of familiarity with the vocabulary of democracy, being in the military, and by the time it was transposed to broken Arabic and hand signs, a lot was lost. The leaflets showing Iraqi tank commanders which way to turn their turrets to live were much more effective. Democracy may be the way to go, but it's not the only way: more than 160 types of government have been identified by some guy on the Web, and while angelocracy, chiliarchy (government by exactly 1,000 people), fool-ocracy, and strumpetocracy don't seem to be contenders, others are.

Oligarchy can work, although it's not for everybody. Contrary to popular belief, it does not mean, necessarily, rule by three. That's severalocracy. A few could be fifty, something to keep in mind the next time someone wants to borrow a few dollars. At least three (two being a biarchy) and less than a thousand, let's say. Eleven, hende-carchy, is a good number, particularly in numerology, and in other places might be considered a minion. The exact number is not as important as finding quality individuals with useful skills who are willing to be expunged if things don't go as expected (it's hard to attract and keep good people where people vote with their Kalash-nikovs). Feudalism has pretty much had its day, and although his-torically important, its cottage industries, no matter how inviting the labor costs, are not for today's marketplace; the other extreme, corpocracy, rule by Halliburton and Bechtel, has its own downside, particularly if you're a local bidder for goods and services. A puppet state sounds a lot cuter than it turns out to be: Vichy, not Tooner-ville. General Ky is not still around, but I bet some of the uniforms are, although that didn't turn out ideal (as we say around here). A puppet inevitably wants to be a real boy, and blue fairies are few and far between.

You have to like the sound of a meritocracy; it's too bad it turns out to be civil service and thus has nothing to do with merit. A theocracy, God, I hope not. Socialism hasn't worked yet, but neither has anything else, and it *is* important to share. Autocracy smacks of Plutocracy, and an orange dog already lords it over me. I suppose a benevolent dictatorship, given the previous administration, would be out of the question, but it would be worth asking Paul Wolfowitz, who should be ratcheting down about now, if he'd consider it. There's nothing wrong with a monarchy, except in England, and they'll be all right once they get past the Windsors. The King of Ur, from these parts, was very well respected in his day and did much to put the civil in civilization, not a bad tradition to harken back to. Wouldn't have to be a king, necessarily, could be a padishah, a caliph, a nawab, or an emir. Then you could have an emirate like the United Arabs have, with those elaborate resorts. An emirate sounds like money in the bank.

Anarchy, while fine at first, quickly descends into a way of doing things, and then it's only a matter of time before you find yourself in an adhocracy. I personally could live in an adhocracy, but my wife would hate it, for what that's worth. Should you have no government to speak of and find that things still run under their own inertia, it would shake the very foundations of the modern state and the Heritage Foundation in particular. Kakistocracy, rule by the worst, goes universally unrecommended, if intentionally. If things just turn out that way, it's time to get serious about the kind of government you want.

54

The Moving Mouth, Having Spoke, Moves On

I'm a talker, not a writer. There, I said it, and I'm glad. Why put down on paper what anybody and your brother can pore over for every inaccuracy and supposed nuance when you could blurt much the same thing and apologize for it later if need be? One thing you can say for the spoken word: say it, it goes away, although it may show up later in a transcript (gone are the days; however, ten cents in coin would get you one from the Merkle Press). Like the Bee Gees, you can always claim they're only words. The verbal keeps things light; Schwarzenegger admires Hitler in writing, it's an endorsement. A paper trail, they call it, and for good reason. There are exceptions—Homer was right to dictate the *Iliad* because his daughters, no matter how many times they heard the stories, could not be depended upon to get it right, and, gods forbid it should be left to his wife's recollection.

In real life, I mean the one that's still not a reality show, I hardly talk at all, having little opportunity in a household with three women who lack the low-gain antennae necessary to receive the weak male signal and coming into work and going to the tavern only once (or twice) a week, those being the only other places I'm likely to volunteer an observation. Other than that, I have to cram in everything I have to say in two hours a week on the radio, although the last thirty minutes is usually musical fill. Sometimes I must give the impression of not wanting to communicate at all, at least to my wife, if I read her lips correctly (sometimes the snarl gets in the way). Communication may not be a high priority with me. If I were in the hole and heard the dirt starting to rattle the cherry (nice, but not top of the line) box they got me, I might say something and I might not. I wouldn't want to start a whole *thing*. It would be bad enough hearing what the rabbi (the kid, really, the old man [a saint!] having been gone for years), talking through his beaver hat, had to say about me. I could never communicate again and not miss it. Maybe I would. Like drugs, it's all set and setting; you know, when you're young and desperately seeking biological advantage, you listen, with a mix of real or simulated interest, to all the partial insights and dubious assessments that a pretty young thing who's had more than her share of adversity already in her life brings to the Posturepedic, but should she end up never leaving it, there's not really much more concern you can summon, except that you really need to get some sleep. Communication being a two-way street, the inverse occurs, too: first they hang on every word, then every other word, but in the end you surely hang alone.

I didn't take Com Arts in college, so not only don't I know what it is I do, technically; I never learned why humans communicate beyond tics and dumb show. If cave drawings are any indication, it has something to do with bison. Once the bison are gone, there appears to come a long epoch, which we're still slogging through, when there isn't much to add, really, just the same old same old. Man spent pre-history learning how to talk and then, once he discovered that whatever he said would be used against him, clammed up during history. It's been that way ever since. In terms of personal history, I remember having the urge to express myself, but that was the '70s for you; like the denim leisure suit, the earth shoes, and the mutton chops; I'm embarrassed about it retroactively. That drive peaked about the time my feminism did (although I still trot out my female side, occasionally), at least that part of me that asked the remainder "Okay, as a woman, how do I feel about this?" By the Reagan years, I was wondering how I would feel about things were I a man. Now, I don't wonder either way. I think I would have had misgivings no matter what gender I turned out to be. Maybe I'm just a private person, who, for some reason, feels compelled to go public. Dad was never dubbed the Great Communicator, either, but we got the gist of his asides, and he always would insert "follow me?" or "understand what I'm saying?" even when there was no way you couldn't, so you've got to give him that. They're just now learning how insects communicate, and, one day, they may discover how Feldmans do it—secretions, I would venture, in both cases, picked up, in the Feldman, by receptors in the eye glass frames. It leaves you shaking your head at the ingenuity of nature, or for other reasons.

55

Afterword

The Secret of Life, Revealed

It says here that parents, even though they would seem to be afforded many more reasons, are much less likely to kill themselves than nonparents. Obviously, nonparents don't know what they're missing, and parents don't have time to think about what they're missing. You have but to witness your daughter's horror at finding your underwear on the floor to know you'd like to avoid her ever finding Dad crumpled up next to the hamper. Not that I'd ever seriously consider it, although, to be honest, while the girls have been my antidepressants, I do get down once in a while, not maybe to the fifth sublevel of the underground structure but to the lobby, or maybe 1G, forgetting that I didn't bring my car. I've always tended that way; if you can imagine a little kid who wonders why he has to go to Steuben Junior High School that morning when we all die in the end, you'll have me. I'm kind of a manic-depressive who doesn't believe in extremes. A whiff of melancholy there is about me. And while fifty-four years may not be all that many, tell it to John Ritter, Robert Palmer, or Whitey from *Leave It to Beaver,* all taken from us at just that age, in an untimely, but just barely, fashion. It does give one menopause.

One of the questions audience members most frequently write on the cards we have them fill out is "What is the secret of life?" (the others are "What's the one question you get most tired of being asked?" ("This one!") and "Do you cut your own hair?"—yes, ever since a barber in Kenosha laughed at how it corkscrews this way and that in 1974. Then the dentist goes and laughs at my teeth.). Let me get to ultimate meaning in a minute (they probably asked it as a joke, like "boxers or briefs?" but it's caused me to think about it over the years, if just to finally have something to say, and I'm just about there). First, let me say that since I will probably never have the chance to write another book (unless, of course, you've ordered 10 or 15,000 of these to give out as presents), this may be the only chance I'll have to add anything or forever hold my peace. It's a lot of pressure, man. I feel, for example, that I should say something about my relationship with Wife No. 2 to make you understand why I seem to convey certain attitudes that cause some people to ask "Does your wife listen to the show?" and others to assume I'm kidding. But she makes a very nice impression, and you wouldn't believe me, anyway, so why bother? I hope that things work out for her, eventually. If, one day, she happens to make another mistake, I will not have been the only one, and I will be released from that particular circle of karma. As for me, a fortune teller once told me I would get three balls for a quarter, so, who knows, I may have another ball coming. Come to think of it, it may have been the carney in the next booth over who said that, and I've been living with false hope.

When you're young, it's all about what you can do for yourself or what your country can do for you, but, with kids, it's entirely what you can do for them. In the end, which is where it gets you, it still beats perfecting your lifestyle, what with the price of rugs. You can't expect your pets to carry on a little part of you, unless you keep big cats, so I guess I'm talking legacy here. I love having daughters; they make me feel that evolution is still occurring, not only having gone beyond the male (something I've parted with only reluctantly) but being inherently free of the limitations, self-doubts, and predispositions you've tried everything to get out of your best things and failed. They may achieve what you and I were unable to, like George W. was able to do for George I, but it's more likely they'll find their own limitations, which you, in some way, may have enabled them to see beyond to things they were meant to do that will sustain them. I don't know how the elder Mr. Bush feels, but I wouldn't want my kids to finish what I've begun—I'm sorry I even began most of it. Some things are best left undone; others, somebody else could probably do better. Some I'm still working on. Some turned out pretty well, but nothing as well as them. As their father, I would like them to know that I will always be there for them, just like the Mustafa-shaped cloud in *The Lion King*. I still turn to my parents often, partly through metaphysics but mostly just by acknowledging the mom and dad within. Maybe, someday, my kids will do what I do: when you sneeze, say "Hi, Dad!" and when you hiccup, "Hi, Mom!"

That, as far as I've been able to tell, is the secret of life.